DETOUR

DETOUR

My Bipolar
Road Trip in 4-D

◆

Lizzie Simon

ATRIA BOOKS
New York London Toronto Sydney Singapore

ATRIA BOOKS, a division of Simon & Schuster, Inc.
1230 Avenue of the Americas, New York, NY 10020

Library of Congress Cataloging-in-Publication Data

Simon, Lizzie.
    Detour : my bipolar road trip in 4-D / Lizzie Simon.
       p. cm.
    ISBN 0-7434-4659-3 (alk. paper)
       1. Simon, Lizzie.   2. Manic-depressive illness—Patients—United
States—Biography.   3. Manic-depressive illness—Popular works.
    I. Title.

    RC516.S56 2002
    616'89'5'50092—dc21
    [B]
                                                    2001060261

First Atria Books hardcover printing June 2002

10   9   8   7   6   5   4   3   2   1

ATRIA is a trademark of Simon & Schuster, Inc.

For information regarding special discounts for bulk purchases,
please contact Simon & Schuster Special Sales at 1-800-456-6798
or business@simonandschuster.com

Designed by Jaime Putorti

Printed in the U.S.A.

My research for *Detour* was supported in part through a grant from the National Federation of Families for Children's Mental Health.

Detour is a true story, although some names and details have been changed.

acknowledgments

I first want to thank my parents and brothers and grandmothers and extended family for all of the support and encouragement they gave me for this project. Thank you, thank you, thank you.

And there were many many other helpers. Barbara Huff, thank you, for your incredible generosity and faith. Thank you Nan Graham and Mark Costello for taking such good care of me. Thank you Kim Witherspoon for taking me on and not giving up. Thank you Alexis Hurley: I would never have finished the book without you. Thank you Greer Kessel Hendricks, for your amazing confidence and vision and determination. Thank you Judith Curr, Karen Mender, Tracy Behar, Seale Ballenger, and Suzanne O'Neill as well. Thank you Sylvie Rabineau.

I would like to thank everybody who put me up and put up with me while I was on the road, and I would like to thank all of the people I interviewed for the book, those who made the cut and those who didn't.

Thank you Dorie Ellsion. Thank you Mindy K. Thank you Phyllis Raphael, Greg Mottola, and Kevin Corrigan. Thank you

Angela Davis and Patty Duke. Thank you Bob Dylan and Stevie Nicks.

Thank you Geoff. Thank you to the Malloys. Thank you Holly and George. Thank you Barry Marshall. And thank you John Berendt.

Thank you also to Tim McCarthy, Anne Washburn, Blake Nelson, Simon Hammerstein, Jim Simpson, Jan Leslie Harding, Steve Greco, Galaxy Craze, the Berensons, the Glassmans, the Kafkos, the Lewis Family, the Gresh-McGinns, the Keisners, Robert Kessel, Joey Xanders, Maya White, Stephanie Jillian, Laurie Stone, Timothy Speed Levitch, Mike Albo, Anne Douglas, and Shela Halper.

Thank you LAVA, Spyralforce, WKCR 89.9 FM, Marymount Manhattan College, the Wellfleet Public Library, the Columbia men's swim team circa 1994–98, and the kids from Nauset Regional High School.

Thank you Genevieve, Katie, Neha, Kira, Ngina, Dominique, Garrett, Tildy, RJ, Theresa, Bethany, Gina, and Julia.

And thank you MF, for the good stuff.

Get Lost! The head of the herd said to Elmer.

Poor Elmer. Everybody wants him to get lost.

One day he got an idea. He would start to walk and keep walking.

So one day he did.

Finally he found another herd and they all had the same problem.

The End

Lizzie Simon, age seven

part

1

It all started the day after I had been accepted for early admission to Columbia College.

December 19, 1993.

I was seventeen years old.

I had left my family at home in Providence, Rhode Island, and was attending my senior year of high school abroad at an international school in Paris. I was having a great time, living with friends of my parents, Edgar and Linda Phillips.

Wait.

I don't remember everything that happened.
Some memories I've forgotten over time.
Some events I blocked out as soon as they happened.
And I suppose it didn't start on that exact day,
that it started in high school,
or before,
much before maybe,
at birth,
or pre-birth; it started with my grandfather, who had this illness, or with the relative of his who passed it along to him.
Wait. Stop.

What started the day after I found out I was accepted to college was an episode so horrific that it would become impossible for me to deny that I had a mental illness for the rest of my life.

Though I had always known that something was wrong with me, what started that day was evidence, concrete evidence.

Yes. True.

Hold on. Rewind.

The history of the inside of my head is the hardest to tell, because it is nonlinear, because it is fractured, because there are so many subplots, and because I have spent so much of my energy in my young life hiding that history from the outside world.

I was born on March 23, 1976, and was loved immediately by many many daring and dazzling people. First, by my mother and father. Imagine her a stunning and leggy rebel, and him a quiet and good-natured community man. She is a sex expert, a college administrator, a coordinator with Haitian Voodoo priests in their native land and tongue, a marathon runner. He is a pediatrician, a Little League baseball coach, a napper.

My parents' mothers are extraordinary women. My mother's mother was a lifetime social worker, who chased people off the dunes near her summer home in Cape Cod, and made quilts, and supported public radio, and recycled, like, decades before anyone else, and read revolutionary poetry, and worried angrily about everything but loved me with tremendous ferocity from moment one. Those hugs! Would my ribs make it through her hugs! She is still alive, though currently in very advanced stages of dementia.

My father's mother is a hot-shot theater producer. Her father and uncle started the dance hall Roseland in Philadelphia and New York City, so she grew up around nightclubs and live per-formance. She can be a mean lady; don't cross her or be silly or forget for a moment who you are dealing with, but oh the soft spot . . . when I turned one she wrote me a birthday card: "Have your mother show you this when you're older and I make more sense to you: My love for you is irrational and uncategorical." As a teenager I spent many summers living with her. Our relation-ship is intense and spirited.

My mother's father died of a sudden heart attack when he was thirty-eight. My mother was eight years old at the time.

My father's father was a very successful orthopedic surgeon

and involved community man. He was also bipolar, but our family kept it a secret. He was diagnosed the year I was born. I was diagnosed the year he died. We passed the baton.

Before he was treated, he would buy property manically in Florida or take outrageous trips into the ocean on his boat. His depressions were severe and terrifying for my grandmother, my aunt, and my father.

Like everybody else on the planet, my parents are not perfect people, nor are they perfect parents. But they loved me—I'm sure of it—from conception on forward to today. And they love each other, madly. They travel together and listen closely to each other and launch each other off into the world the way young lovers would.

I was loved and looked after by my older brother, Aaron, who was a prodigiously talented athlete and daredevil (at three he dove off of the Olympic-height diving platform at Brown University . . . yes, yes, an insight into my parents: they let him, they launch us too). And then later, eight years after me later, there came Ben, who seemed to emerge into the world in a cheery and mindful Buddha-like state, which he remains in now, even as a teenager. I taught him to talk and to walk, and when he mastered that, I made him dance and sing.

The atmosphere in my house growing up was always exciting and upbeat. During the week, we had dinner together every single night. My parents insisted. On weekends, my mom and dad blasted their rock and roll or folk or soul music from the moment they woke up. At parties, they were the first and last on the dance floor (my dad can actually do this thing where he swings my mother to either side of his hips and then dramatically above his head and into the air). We seemed to have an enormous network of friends from all over the world and from different parts of their lives: old hippie radicals from my father's medical student days; students from Brown, where my mom was Dean of Student Life; actors from the theater where my nana worked. Our home more often than not had guests.

I was a child actress from the age of three to thirteen, so I received an enormous amount of attention from my family and their friends. Show me your latest commercial! Lizzie, sing that Johnny One Note song!

There's so much more. Great-aunts and uncles, cousins—there were dozens upon dozens of people ready and loving at my birth and around through my childhood and adolescence. All of them intense, complicated, but gentle. They are artists and dancers and writers; they are bankers and doctors and college professors.

My family was spread in New York and Los Angeles and Providence and Brazil. We seemed willing to go any distance for a wedding, a bar mitzvah, a reunion, an event. There was always gossip and secrets upstairs and children downstairs making up a show.

My great-aunt Ruth, the matriarch, told me at one meeting of the annual Kissing Cousins Brunch (which only the female members can attend) that mine was "a good generation." And we are. My cousins are all fun, loving, and creative. We are noisy, and we laugh hard. We make time for one another. And we have inherited our parents' and grandparents' gentle and protective nature.

In my family, and extended family, we might each of us be a little crazy, but our intentions are pure. We never set out to hurt one another, and so we rarely do.

This is where I come from.

The larger universe, as you might understand, has always seemed unnecessarily brutal.

Paris was wonderful. Knowing that I had successfully escaped my high school in Providence made it all the more delicious.

A beautiful elite private school, Providence Academy is set on a hill with rolling greens and beautiful facilities. I had gone to public school until ninth grade, and after nine years in the public school system, the Academy was a culture shock stranger than any before or since. This tribe I came upon at the age of fourteen, in CB jackets and polo shirts, had the oddest and most fierce codes of conduct for itself.

I suppose I was an insider, but I never felt that way. I was invited to all of the parties. I was friends with the right people. I dated popular guys—but I never really got it. The ski trips. The parties where no one danced. The humor. The arrogance. The racism and homophobia. Everybody agreed about everything. Lacrosse players were demigods, kids drove Beamers, and the coolest guys in my class pissed on one of the most popular girls at a party our sophomore year. They were the sons and daughters of the wealthiest businessmen, doctors, lawyers, and Mafia leaders in Rhode Island. Everyone was imitating what prep school should be and had always been. But none of it came naturally to me.

I was stuck. I had begged my parents to go there because my older brother attended. Understanding the financial sacrifice they were making, I couldn't possibly complain.

Little ole me, who grew up in a politically radical and charged household. Who had kept a journal of her feelings every day since kindergarten. Who had performed professionally as an actress since she was three, spending a better chunk of her childhood missing school, surrounded by artists. Who still suffered, despite at least a dozen therapeutic interventions dating back to almost prelingual times, from intense and inexplicable mood swings.

Wait. . . .

Okay.

By my sophomore year, I had started dating this really popular boy named Chace Metcalf. He was a junior, but his friends immediately accepted me into their clan. It was not a serious relationship. We were not intimate emotionally or sexually. Actually, I think he was in love with someone else the entire time we went out: a girl who was away at boarding school. By my junior year our relationship was over, but my fixation on him had just begun.

I obsessed over him. It shames me to remember hundreds of pages of Chace journal entries, hours of conversations with friends on the subject, and countless futile attempts to resurrect what had only been a limp connection in the first place.

Chace was never cruel to me, but he didn't need to be.

I tortured myself.

Well, wait. . . .

My depression and anxiety used Chace as a tool for their torture. It's hard to read my journals from that period because I kept writing how much I hated myself. At the time I decided, with what felt like clarity, that Providence Academy was doing me in. I needed to escape.

I devoted myself to completing my credits in three years and convincing my parents to let me go to Paris to finish high school.

I think I was happier in Paris than ever before.

My French school was like college—you didn't have to be there nine to five. I would wake when needed, pack my bag for the day, and walk past the high-class hookers on the corner to the Metro. I'd ride ten minutes to school, passing views of the Eiffel Tower. I would spend my free time wandering around or sitting in cafés smoking and drinking coffee.

No one in Paris had ever heard of lacrosse or Winter Solstice Balls or the Sophomore Girls Posse.

It was my first taste of power, the power I had within me to change my conditions to better my life. I had a lot of freedom, a lot of time on my hands. I felt attractive, intellectually stimulated, adventurous. I thought myself naive and unknowing in so many areas—international politics, French culture, sex. I was always in a position of learning, and it was comfortable. I just learned a lot every day. I understood only half of every French conversation; I relied on my new school friends and Linda to let me know when something was due or when I had to be somewhere.

I have always enjoyed the company of adults, and my relationship with Linda Phillips was very important to me. When I got home from school she asked me how my day was, and we'd sit in the kitchen and talk. We discussed everything—our families, the neighbors, sex, politics. Linda is really smart and has a mind for personalities, so it's her pleasure to chat for an hour and analyze a friendship or a boy situation. She really took me in as a peer, brought me to parties, took me out shopping. She was fun. The neighbors would be changing, and she'd turn off all the lights and we'd watch.

My new friends were fabulous. I had a theater class, and we were required to go see a show every week. Franklin and I would get stoned beforehand and then walk around the city. Tildy had lived her whole life moving every three to five years—DC, Mali, Haiti, Paris. She called herself a global nomad. These kids had stories; they had been around the world and had had intellectual people at their dinner tables their whole lives. They read; they went to museums. They had theories about history, about America, about just about anything.

I remember going to a nightclub on a school night with the whole gang of girls. It was sadomasochism night, and Bethany wore a skin-tight black dress and jumped up on a speaker and gyrated away as soon as we got there. I wrote in my journal that she danced like a cheap whore and that I couldn't wait to go out with her again. Those were things you wouldn't find Carter Danforth doing back in Rhode Island. But my new friends knew about freedom.

I really felt that I belonged. The social rules were lax. There was no dress code. No one wore fancy clothes, or hip clothes. We just put clothes on.

I was enjoying the adventure only an urban locale can provide, and time was flying. I remember thinking I had never been this happy for this long my whole life.

Stop.

And then I got into college. And everything was perfect. For just a moment, a few hours really, a morning. And then I went insane.

I remember walking slowly through the courtyard of my school in Paris, and I remember seeing Tildy through the window. She had heard the news, and she was waving fiercely. I remember Franklin telling me that I wore a shit-eating grin all through English class later that day.

I remember a little fuzz building in my head that made Paris a bit grayer than it was already.

I remember attributing the fuzz to my achievement.

I remember I felt uncomfortable, as if my jeans were too tight and my shoes too big, but in my head.

"I'm having troubles expressing myself to people," the last entry of my journal reads. "Maybe I don't know what I mean. It's hard to remember the beginning of my sentence now that I'm all the way at the end."

I remember thinking, why were things off when I had just gotten into college? I mean, I had worked my whole life for this.

The spiraling of my logic was getting more severe, chasing conclusions at quicker and quicker paces, while my actual articulation was getting slower and slower. I remember feeling I could not say much at all that would be right.

And I remember Linda explaining it away. I was going home the next day anyway, and Linda always thought that I had some pretty seriously mixed-up feelings about my family. She, of course, had some pretty mixed-up feelings about my family. I remember that. But I was going to Providence, and I remember reassuring myself that these circles would diminish once I was on domestic territory.

I remember the pit in my stomach, *no thanks*. I remember not wanting to go out for the celebratory dinner Linda and Edgar proposed.

When I woke the next morning, it was time to leave. I remember the plane ride well. I remember being very Linda in

French blue jeans and the right shoes and jewelry and a blue sweater that I still have. I remember it covered my butt, and Linda thought that was a good thing. I remember the nervousness hadn't disappeared; in fact, I remember wondering why it was getting worse. I was jittery, worried, riddled with anxieties that created paradox laid over paradox. I don't remember what it was all about, really, but just that the load was getting more and more burdensome.

I remember it was the kind of plane where the last row was a smoking section. I sat there next to a guy about my age. My first impression was that he was probably on drugs. He looked raggedy; his hair was blond, long, and stringy; his face was scruffy. He looked skinnier than he should be, and he had a drink in hand. It was the kind of flight where you could have an unlimited number of cocktails, and he and I drank quite a bit during the flight. He certainly didn't fit the composite of the people Linda wanted me around. Where had he been in Paris, and why hadn't I been there?

He broke the ice. "You know," he said, "the most interesting people I have ever met were in the smoking sections of airplanes."

"Really?" I asked, giggling, not fashioning myself as all that interesting.

He was an artist, and he said he had been bumming through Paris.

Eventually he revealed that he had gone to a prep school near my house. So we were from the same place, going back home. And I was getting drunk, and feeling much better about life. His sense of humor was spastic and offbeat, and my vision of reality was already morphing, so he was pleasantly perfect. He was my first relief. We flirted and teased the stewards. He made fun of me, and I gazed at him. I told him he looked like Kurt Cobain. We sat half in our seats, half slumped to the floor of the plane, hurling out irreverences. We smoked and smoked and smoked. His eyes were very, very blue, and I felt safe with him, and I believe he saw my confusion. He moved liked a caterpillar, and he was fuzzy like one too, though now when I imagine him I see a halo. He churtled in and out of my space, and I wanted him to kiss me. Before we got off the plane, we exchanged phone numbers.

Now I was drunk and a bit elated in love when I found my mother and told her I had just met the man of my dreams. He slithered over, reeking of liquor and cigarettes, all dirty and gangly, and met my mom. She said he had an ephemeral quality to him. I thought she meant effeminate, but she said no, she meant, uh, heavenly.

After that point things start to fade, because I slept very late the next day, and I just don't remember much at all until memories of sobbing in bed, and memories of leaving a Christmas party. And I was drifting and drowning, disappointed that I couldn't muster up the enthusiasm to call my friends from home. I was worried about being worried, about having no energy. The walls swooned, and my journals emitted passages about previous depressions until that was all I could remember: suicide attempts at prepubescent intervals, broken-hearted letters, other tears, other darknesses. I had never been so tortured; I felt a mass of pain at every instant, and it was deepening, thickening. I could not speak of it because I had lost the consciousness needed to identify that something was wrong.

Lizzie ended. I was something else, and I had no appreciation of the past or any other present. The way it was those days, it seemed as if that was all I had ever been.

And in the middle of this, my parents were annoyed. They said I was so antisocial, so mopey. What the hell was my problem? And when Tom, the boy from the plane, called I wouldn't pick up the phone. My mother forced me to call him back. He kept wondering what was wrong. I said my family was bugging me. He was coming the next day, and he wanted me to show him Providence.

He picked me up, and we drove around. As it happened, my Providence Academy yearbook inscription copy was due that day, so Tom and I worked on it. Now it is filled with stuff that makes no sense (for example: BNE is cheese), but it ends with our flight number. I couldn't really speak; there were a lot of awkward silences, and I was perennially on the verge of tears, which once begun I feared wouldn't cease for hours. Finally we stopped for lunch. "What's wrong?" he kept asking. I had nothing to say. I felt like such a failure. I felt I had ruined something wonderful.

He, on the other hand, was amazing. Sat with me for a long time in silence, at the beginning of an episode during which people generally terrified me. I was stripped and vulnerable to injury that wasn't actually being inflicted—but if you can understand anything about episodes, see that it was all real for me. But Tom didn't scare me. He sat with me at the window of a sandwich shop, offering to do anything, go anywhere. I said, "Take me home." I broke into tears; I said "sorry" eighteen times; I couldn't hear him any longer. "Please take me home."

He took me home. We went inside, and my mom chatted with him. He said good-bye, I think. I went to my room and sobbed until days later.

The next thing I remember is being driven to a therapist. I sort of felt that I was successfully proving to him how I felt, until he told me that I had been talking in circles for ninety minutes straight, and that I wasn't making a bit of sense, and that I was clinically depressed—so depressed in degrees he had rarely ever seen, and that something absolutely had to be done. With pills. By that point I was a slug, and my dad led my sluggy body to the car, and I probably cried until our next outing on New Year's Eve day to a psychiatrist. The psychiatrist sat with me for a few minutes, asked a few questions, and gave me Paxil, an antidepressant. I'm pretty sure he said that there wouldn't be any side effects. My parents were nervous about my going back to Paris alone. But I convinced everybody to let me. I had exams to complete. I couldn't miss them. And I remember thinking that Providence had caused all of this, anyway.

Things were so strange and dark for me, but I was more worried about taking my finals than I was about taking my Paxil.

My mom dropped me at the airport. She looked tired and frazzled, and I remember thinking that I couldn't say anything to make her feel better about my situation. I remember promising her I'd call a psychiatrist when I got to Paris, though I never did. I remember promising to take my pills, which, of course, I did. And I remember a tremendous body shock when I slammed the door to my mom's car. It had been warm, and the radio had been playing Mary Chapin Carpenter. The door closed. A world rolled off, and I remember feeling alone, cold, and burdened with luggage.

I remember arriving at my friend Gina's in Paris to stay for a couple of weeks while Linda's kids were in town. I sat Gina down and told her I was on antidepressants. I made her swear not to tell her mom and not to tell anyone at school. She promised, and we studied for our next day's math exam. After just two days of Paxil, the pistons in my head had already sped up to normal "Lizzie speed" and were quickly surpassing that level. That night, I made Gina stay up until 5:30 to study math. Even after that, I couldn't sleep. I attributed it to nervousness.

I don't remember anything chronologically, really, until I arrived at Linda's two weeks later in a psychotic state. Only scattered flashes remain.

I remember standing in my English class while we were discussing *The Invisible Man* and sparking a long tirade about how the book was really one line from every famous book ever written, woven together to make sense, but the trick of it was that it makes sense in the beginning, but not at the end. Furthermore, I argued, Ellison constructed it so that no one could possibly get past chapter six. "Has anyone here," I challenged, "gone past chapter six?" And who here can prove that Ellison existed? "Son-of-Ellis," I pointed out. "Son of America's roots." I directed the class to the back of the book, where a reviewer had written that the book belongs on the shelf with all the classics of literature.

"On the shelf," I beamed, electric with my discoveries. "On-the-shelf." My teacher stared at me blankly, as did my classmates. They don't get it, I thought.

In my mind, everyone slowly became complicit in a plot to get me.

And so I remember avoiding people, which is part of why I was psychotic for so long. Gina, being a good friend, kept her promise of secrecy. Perhaps people thought I was drunk, reeling from my early acceptance into college. Perhaps it is part of French culture not to intercede in someone's life if you've only known the person for four months. Perhaps my friends, at age seventeen, were ill equipped to save someone psychotic. It was final exam time of their senior, and most important, year of high school. Perhaps they had other things about which to worry.

I saw men from the CIA when I walked to the Metro. They flashed behind corners, but I always managed to escape them by running. I ran quite a bit. I also avoided their scheme to rape and kill me by not eating. They had contaminated whatever food I could get my hands on. I also didn't sleep, because I couldn't, and because I knew they would capture me if I were to close my eyes. I vaguely remember figuring out that my international school classmates were all hostages, but that I hadn't been fully brainwashed, and that I needed to escape before I became one of them.

A skinny tall girl with big frizzy blond hair stole my lighter to tease me. When she gave it back, I was certain that she was going to kill me so, I lit a cigarette and tried to burn her eye out with it. Someone held me back while she screamed at me in French, calling me a lunatic.

I remember not going to school one day and wandering the streets of Paris, avoiding enemies who approached at every corner.

I remember trying to return to Gina's one night but getting very lost. I don't remember how I got there, but I remember it was extremely late, and Gina was worried when I finally arrived.

I remember going to Linda's one day. The entire family was

away skiing in Switzerland. The apartment was dark, and the concierge's kid, who was three or four, came in with me. It occurred to me that everyone was going to accuse me of molesting him, so I screamed at him and made him leave.

I remember not being able to do a simple exercise in my theater class, because everything had become too confusing.

I remember sitting in a cafe on a sunny day, standing up and announcing that I was going to walk until I got laid.

I remember walking and realizing why the Mona Lisa was smiling. I was figuring out so many things.

I remember sitting in my bedroom at Gina's, and finding that there were microphones everywhere. Many nights I spent in the dark, waiting for killers to arrive.

I remember writing about a dozen letters to semirandom people—teachers from back home, Chace's sister, an old friend with whom I had lost touch. I remember sending those letters.

I remember my last moments at Gina's. I went to the bathroom, and I saw blood on the walls and microphones in the corners of the ceiling. I grabbed my papers filled with manic ramblings into a bag, left a note for Gina pleading with her to try and escape, and ran out of the building. But then I ran into her. She started to cry as I got into the cab, and I told the driver to go to Linda's. I could see Gina on the curb helplessly wiping tears from her cheeks. I can still see her there.

When I arrived, I couldn't find any money. The driver locked the doors and told me to give him a blow job. I started screaming viciously, and he let me out. I ran up to Linda's apartment and told her I needed to escape. I also told her that I was a cat, a realization that had come to me a few days earlier.

I remember that she couldn't get in touch with my parents because they were in Puerto Rico, and there was an earthquake in Puerto Rico. I took those details and understood that the CIA had created disturbances around the world to prevent my escape. Linda made some strange choices. She asked her son, who was a certified EMT, to check my vital signs. I thought he was going to rape me, so I bit down on my hand until it broke the skin. She thought I should take a bath, which seemed like a good idea to me as well, since I was a bug-infested cat. But she locked me in the bathroom, which convinced me that she was out to get me, too. She then locked me in the *chambre de bonne,* a room with no windows on the top floor of the building, a room meant for a maid back in the days when people kept maids in such rooms. In that room I sat wet and terrified. Linda came up and tried to psychoanalyze me, and she was holding a long stick. She then told me she was going to an embassy party, and that I had to come because she couldn't let me stay home alone. Apparently, she couldn't miss an embassy party either.

In my psychotic reality I thought I was the CIA's most wanted cat, and I was being dragged to an embassy party. Soon after we arrived, I began embarrassing Linda, so she had Edgar walk me home.

I was just about to jump off the terrace in a suicide attempt when the phone rang. It was a woman who sounded just like my mother, but I knew that it was probably the CIA, so I pretended I was Linda. My mother was really confused, and was clearly distraught that Linda had left me alone in the apartment.

Linda eventually returned. On advice from the American Hospital in Paris, I stopped taking the Paxil that night. Linda informed me that the pills proved I had something called bipolar disorder, which I thought meant that I was a hermaphrodite. But that still only began to explain to me why I had turned into a cat.

The next morning Linda and Edgar took me to the airport. I had packed a bag full of schoolbooks and journals. These items seemed most important for my survival, and I had to keep them from the CIA. The books, if found by the wrong people, would ensure my extermination. If I could get them into the right hands, I could usher in the revolution. It was a very heavy bag. I was pleased when we arrived at the airport, for I had been certain all night that they were plotting to send me to a boarding school in the north of France. Linda bought my ticket, and a small Asian woman led me to the plane. The horror struck me, my most terrifying realization so far: the plane was going either to a prison in Siberia, or to hell, and all of the people on the plane were in my condition.

The people on the plane were very odd. Most were drenched with sweat and seemed sickly and disturbed. Almost every person on the plane was wearing an article of my clothing, and in their hands they held my belongings—my books, my journals, my pictures. The flight attendants were rubbing their fingers around my pills, and overhead the sounds of more pills dropping on the ceiling menaced me.

I couldn't sit still.

I tried at one point to open the emergency door, but a flight attendant grabbed my arms and sent me back to my seat.

There was always blood on my pillow, so I kept trying to move. But it seemed as if every chair I sat in presented another problem.

When we were served a meal, there were rat feet markings in my food and hairs sticking out of the beef.

One man told me I needed to take my shirt off, so I began to.

In the bathroom, there were cameras hovering overhead and inside the toilet. If I was going to relieve myself, I would have to suffer the humiliation of everybody on the plane seeing my peeing from both angles. I really had to go, so I did, but I let everybody on the plane have it as I returned to my seat. By the end of the trip, everybody knew who I was, and I let them know that I knew exactly what was going on.

Near the end of the flight, I asked one man where we were going.

"Boston," he said. Yeah, right, I thought.

I remember I wouldn't fill out the embarkation card because there was no box to mark "cat" under gender. I ranted and screamed my way through customs somehow, and then I saw my grandmother waiting. I was elated: I had escaped.

I was really excited that evening. I was bug infested, but I was home and in America. Surely my father, the doctor, would know where and how to decontaminate me once he got back to the house. Plus, I had just accomplished some sort of international hijinks, and it was just a matter of time before the entire country would begin heralding my terrific feats.

For the time being, though, my grandmother offered to defrost me some pea soup from the freezer. I declined, showered, and got into bed.

I don't really remember much at all after that, but I know what my mother remembers.

She says that by midnight they had returned from Puerto Rico. I had fallen asleep, which was good. I hadn't really slept for weeks. When I woke in the morning, my mother was asleep on the floor beside my bed. She says I woke her up and demanded she find *Backlash,* by Susan Faludi. I wasn't angry, she says, just incredibly determined.

My mother raced about the house and found the book. I opened it up to a certain section, and handed the book back to my mother. Then I proceeded to recite the book, as if from memory, to my mother. Whole chunks, she says, line by line.

My mom says there was a moment when she first woke up that morning that I seemed so normal, and that even through the recitations of feminist literature she thought, hey listen—this isn't too bad. She's alive, she's not violent or suicidal, she's almost making sense, she's in our care, we're going to get her help . . . this is almost over, I think she thought.

I overhead things during moments of lucidity. My mom and dad felt Linda and Edgar were irresponsible for not accompanying me home. My mom was so angry and my dad was so sad.

Linda called and told me my mother and father were irresponsible for not telling her I was on psychiatric drugs.

I was supposed to tell you, I thought. *Everybody stop fighting. I'm responsible.*

Linda and I were never really friends again.

My parents didn't hospitalize me. It turned out that I was

toxic and psychotic from the Paxil, a drug that can induce mania in bipolar patients. I had to be brought down—and they have lovely drugs for that. Drugs that erase your memory, drugs that make you drool, drugs that drain your brain. One or both of my parents stayed home with me during the time the antipsychotics did their deal.

I imagine the brain like an outer space cosmos, with little ships and beams of light zipping around carrying messages and directives. I imagine my universe at the time in utter chaos, and the antipsychotics as a nuclear bomb. Like we haven't developed humane sophisticated ways to deal with disorder, so let's melt the whole thing down.

Stop.

I started lithium about a week later. I really didn't want to take it, but things were beginning to get really bad again, depression-wise.

I was terrified.

I was told I should go on it for the rest of my life, that bipolar disorder is a chronic mental illness that only worsens with age. It sounded very serious. Lithium? Forever? Could I be *that* sick? What had happened didn't seem like an episode. It seemed like a permanent change, a series of life-altering events in which I would forever be held prisoner. I had been transformed into a raving lunatic in Paris and then into an antipsychoticized heap of skin, floating around like a ghost. What next?

Lithium. I imagined zombies in loony bins. I imagined wealthy pill-popping housewives. I imagined indie rockers. Get her on lithium. Get some lithium flowing through her. Poke the lithium stick through her and set her on the grill like a shish kebab. Lithium. What would it turn me into? That was the big question. Look what Paxil had done, and that was just an anti-depressant. Lithium was a very serious-sounding drug. It sounded so sinister. And any reassurance of its safety sounded like nonsense. I didn't exactly trust my doctor or my parents. LOOK WHAT HAPPENED THE LAST TIME YOU CONVINCED ME TO TAKE A DRUG YOU MOTHERFUCKERS.

I figured they'd keep me on the third floor of our house and let me waste away without hurting anybody. I'd be the crazy uncle in the attic. My parents would have guests over, and they'd bring me downstairs. This is *Lizzie.* Hi Lizzie, the perfumed guests would say, and on the way home they'd discuss what a shame it was what happened to me and how kind and good the Simons were for not sending me away somewhere far far away. LOOK WHAT HAPPENED TO ME YOU ASSHOLES, LOOK AT ME, LOOK WHAT HAPPENED WITH YOUR FUCK-ING PILLS. And that had been only a few weeks ago. Lithium. Didn't Kurt Cobain write a song called "Lithium"? Stick her on lithium; it'll calm her down. Take the lithium. Swallow, sweetheart. It was so menacing.

But lithium worked for me. Just two days on lithium, and I was fine by most people's standards. Lucid, calm, sleeping regularly, eating regularly. Not crazy, not at all.

There were side effects for six months, and then the side effects began to diminish until they disappeared. At first there were headaches—unreal, world-deafening headaches. And thirst. Oh, thirst like you've never known. I had to have water around at all times. And the shakes—my hands would shake; it would weird people out. I gained twenty-five pounds and developed a lot of acne.

I looked like a different person. I felt like one, too.

People talk about psychopharmaceuticals changing their personalities, dulling them down, or overmellowing them. I did not notice those changes.

The changes I noticed were the result of the depressive and manic events in Paris and Providence. I felt different. I had lost faith in my parents, Linda and Edgar, my friends, the medical community, God, the time-space continuum, my memory, my brain, my body, my eyes and ears, my heart, and my soul.

Lithium gave me a functional brain.

But now I had heavy and intense shame, doubts, and fears.

Lithium didn't know how to take care of that.

I didn't either.

I remember that period of time as if it were my second birth.

I died when I went crazy in Paris, and started over when I was diagnosed and put on lithium.

I started over, from scratch, at seventeen.

My parents made me go back to school about two weeks after I had returned from Paris. I did not feel ready; the drugs hadn't even settled in. And Providence Academy was the most terrifying place on earth for me. Going back was the ultimate surrender to the power of the illness. I hated that place. I had escaped, and then something enormous and terrible and mysterious happened. And I had to go back there.

I remember my mother called an old friend of mine named Mindy and had her visit me at our house the night before I was to return to school. Mindy and I had gone to preschool together and had remained best friends until we were teenagers, when Mindy began her descent into anorexia and our connection dwindled. Mindy had already been in and out of hospitals, but she was back at Providence Academy, struggling still. She stood before me at a reasonable weight. She looked at me in kindness and friendship.

"What do I tell people?" I moaned to her.

She shrugged her shoulders. "Mitigating circumstances," she offered. "It works pretty good. Mitigating—you know, most people at Providence Academy get thrown off by the word 'mitigating.'"

I remember my first day back at school. My morning class had gone all right. Nice people, nice teacher.

But now I have a free period. I enter the student center. Everybody's looking at me; everybody's asking why I'm back in Providence. I can't keep my stories straight, and I know people are talking. I retract. I have a homework assignment from my first class: I'm supposed to read an article. I take it from my bag, but I can't read it. The words are jumping all over the page. I look up in despair, and people are looking at me. Nobody sits alone in the student center. I sit clutching the photocopied article, pretending to read it, holding on for dear life.

But I can't read.

I can't talk to anybody.

I can't do anything.

Can I get someone to come pick me up? I wonder desperately. I can't do this. . . .

For some reason, an image pops into my mind. I remember belting out show stoppers in my preadolescence for large audiences to thunderous applause. I was a real hit on the talent show circuit, even though my mom refused me the gaudy costumes and adult makeup. The other girls could toe-tap or climb stairs on their hands; I only had a decent voice but huge unexpected performance balls. *Johnny only had one note to sing and the note he sang was this: AAAAAAAAAAAAAAHHHHHHHHH!!!!!!!!!!!!*

I was afraid of nothing. Was that still in me? How could I get that back?

Lithium wasn't the only drug that helped me recover after I was diagnosed with manic depression. Eventually I was smoking pot about five times a day, hanging out with an ebullient Campbell soup–looking kid who dealt most of the drugs in our school. The first time I tried marijuana I worried that it might shatter my mental health completely. But when nothing happened except the general dopiness that one expects from weed, I realized that I wasn't quite as fragile as I had previously thought.

I was a pothead for six months. And thank God. It put me into the hands of a bunch of really nice kids who were nonthreatening, creative, musical, and accepting of a new person. I had never been friends with these people before, because my friends were always older and they had graduated. So we'd drive around during free periods and get high, and I had seventeen thousand free periods because everybody was afraid of giving me too big a work load and stressing me out.

I needed to be high all the time because I couldn't deal with the intensity of what had happened to me in Paris, I couldn't deal with my parents, and most of all I couldn't stand being back in high school. For me, pot was a bridge back to real life, a cushiony warm soft bridge that made the day-to-day OK while my brain and body adjusted to lithium and while my soul began to digest the trauma. Also, pot made it easy to be social again after the most alienating and horrifying experience of my life. When I started smoking pot and hanging out with potheads, I felt normal, age appropriate.

I didn't feel like a sick kid.

I didn't feel like the Big Burden.

I didn't feel dirty and scummy and messy and brimming with toxic waste.

Wait.

Stop.

Mental illness interacts with the way you define yourself from the instant it enters your life. There was a whole seventeen and a half years of living before this horrible episode descended upon me. Seventeen and a half years of wondering why I never felt quite right anywhere. Not in my home, not in my schools, not in my cliques, not with my boyfriends. Did this mental illness thing explain everything that had ever happened to me? Was lithium going to make me more fit for life, for fun, for love?

And who was going to help me deal with what I had been through? Who was going to understand *that?*

In the fall I began college at Columbia in New York City. I would get to start over. New people, new city, new challenges.

Suddenly my parents and I were in a long line to move into my freshman dorm with lots of other nervous eighteen-year-olds and their parents. Not a happy day. By four in the afternoon, I sat my parents down and said that the best and kindest thing they could do for me would be to leave. I had a new roommate to get to know, classes to pick, a cappella group tryouts.

I was back on track.

But it wasn't over. Maybe it seemed to be over, to my parents, to my close friends. It wasn't over.

You can't just hand a bipolar person lithium and be done with her. I mean, you *can*—and that's exactly what's done for most bipolar people. That's how it went for me, anyway. But that's not treatment. That's not good care.

I never got any therapy. I tried, but my therapists weren't bipolar. They didn't understand.

Who was going to understand what I had been through? How was I supposed to figure this all out? My parents wanted me to move on and away from it as fast as I could. And I did, too. I really did. I thought, if I can achieve success, then I will feel OK. The more success I can achieve, the more my haunting memories and my unanswered questions will disappear. I will put all things bipolar to the side, I decided—in the corner, away somewhere.

I spent my freshman year winning friends.

I was relieved to find that I could make and keep friends.

That people really trusted me even if I couldn't reciprocate fully.

That I wasn't the only one using Columbia to start over.

Two of my closest friends, Garrett and Genevieve, lived with me for the remaining years of college. We tried to figure it all out together, and we did, but each of us had our own special stuff in our own special corners. Most of the time, my special stuff didn't feel any larger than anyone else's.

I told my closest friends about my bipolar episodes, but it was tricky. Everybody's heard things about mental illness, seen things on TV, read books with mad characters. Everybody's already got ideas in their head about it.

I waited until I was sure they could handle it, and I figured out the best way to talk about it. I made it palatable, and every single friend I opened up to was great (after I told my friend RJ that I was bipolar, he said "oh" and nodded and confessed to me that he had asthma). I certainly didn't seem moody to them, and revealing issues was sort of "in." But my excessive packaging of the experience usually put me at a greater distance from the person I was talking to, instead of bringing me closer, as I had desired.

Now that I had friends, I tried to regain my intellectual confidence. My first year was academically beguiling; almost everything, it seemed, went over my head. I had very little idea what was being discussed and how it connected to anything else in virtually all of my classes.

In my second year, I found a mentor in a class called "History of the Radical Tradition in America." My professor was brilliant and my graduate student teacher's assistant was brilliant and my section was brilliant. I was totally intimidated, but my teacher's assistant singled me out, took me under his wing, and just said, *I think you're really smart. You have great ideas but you don't express them well. You seem kind of sad. You don't talk much, but you should. What's going on?*

I don't remember what I told him. His name was Tim. He was a devoted teacher and a radical thinker. His lectures were passionate sermons.

Perhaps he intuited that there was great capacity for devotion within me. He started calling on me all the time. I was doing the reading, but I didn't feel that I was really getting it, and I didn't know how to talk like the other kids talked so I would just say whatever came into my head. I would just say why I was confused, and I'd be totally mortified. But Tim would always say something like EXACTLY! with bulging eyeballs, and an intellectual was born within me.

I attended special lectures, pored through rare books, and challenged my conservative dormmates.

Our class extended discussion and debates to the local bars in the area. People in the class started to refer to things I had said— and these were smart people! I was particularly impressed with one student, Josh. He was the smartest kid I had ever met in my entire life. And he thought I was smart! I really couldn't believe it. All of a sudden I was smart again.

Once I felt I had mastered writing papers, taking exams, and doing research, I again felt a space inside of me, an emptiness, a longing.

When a fellow student offered me his position as arts director at the college radio station, I took it.

I had a weekly show and oversaw four other shows in the department.

I went gonzo.

There was once again the learning part of the quest; I had to master engineering, interviewing, and management skills.

But once again, I took something and applied complete devotion to it. Soon I was interviewing Matt Damon, John Waters, Gus Van Sant, Julianne Moore. I was scamming my way into Broadway shows and industry parties. I had indie film stars and young writers stopping by my dorm room to hang out. I produced an arts festival, which featured over one hundred artists; I was on the air for twenty-four hours straight. By senior year, the phone in my dorm room rang so often that I usually kept the ringer off. When Garrett or Genevieve answered, he or she would say, "Lizzie Simon's office."

Graduation lingered there in the ever-approaching future.

I had mastered college, but so what, I thought. I knew I wouldn't have papers to ace and radio shows to produce for much longer. And when graduation day hit, I didn't take it so well.

The night before graduation I cut my hair, which had been long, brown, and curly; it hung two inches beyond my shoulders. I cut it short, like army head short. And I cut it with a huge pair of blunt scissors.

I remember Garrett, Genevieve, and I dressing into our baby-blue caps and gowns. Their dorm rooms were bare and stripped, empty except for full suitcases and stuffed boxes. Mine looked as it had a few months earlier; I hadn't begun to pack.

While my classmates, high as kites, raised the roof all over campus chanting 98! 98! 98! I wrote depressing poetry and sulked.

Garrett said, "Lizzie, I don't know what you're so *upset* about; it's going to be like summer vacation but for the rest of our lives!"

I was afraid of the real world. Afraid of being an adult.

I knew I could find a job, but I needed something to throw my whole self into. I wanted a devotion.

Then Jim Simpson came on my radio show, the very last show I did as a student.

He arrives early. Jim has never listened to WKCR 89.9 FM, so I tell him how it's the greatest station in the universe, and I start to describe all the terrific jazz and new music we broadcast. I'm talking his ear off for maybe three minutes, and he's just listening. Then he asks me what I'm doing after graduation. I tell him I don't know. He asks what would I do if I had a job producing music in his space, the Flea.

Now I don't know anything about music; I'm the arts director. I listen to R&B and hip-hop at home, and when I'm lonely I listen to light favorites. I think my friends would say I have exceptionally cheap taste in music. But I say, well I'd do a jazz series and a Latin series and a New Music series and an African series and an American music series. (Those are the names of the departments at WKCR.) And I would make it interactive, I say. (I'd been watching VH-1.)

I figure some pasty sophomore at the station will help me find the right people, and a jazz DJ legend will help me figure out the bigger conceptual picture, and I can figure out the grunt work.

The theater is really a mess, he warns me; three floors of a building, but no seats, or painted walls. No offices, or finished bathrooms. It is a pit, and no one has heard of it.

This doesn't bother me.

The job is mine. The devotion is beginning.

It's now May, 1999, not quite a year since I graduated from college.

I'm at work, my boss is leaving for vacation soon, and I have to ask him for a raise before he goes.

I don't have to, but I want to and my cousin Brian, the broker, has been coaching me. I'm making $600 a week, and Brian tells me to go for eight.

No matter how much you think you deserve a raise, asking for one is difficult because it requires you to say *I am useful, valuable, and deserving* to a person with the authority to validate you or not. Brian is good with pep talks.

We are on the phone. *He needs you,* he keeps telling me. *He knows it. He knows what everybody says about you; he knows he's damned lucky to have you.*

The theater has been in the papers a lot lately.

Don't undervalue yourself. You just tell him it's what you think you're worth. And $800 is nothing. Nothing.

I think it's a lot, I tell him.

Are you kidding me? he says, exasperated. *Kids from your college at any given firm are making twice that, easy, ten seconds out of school.*

And they're idiots. No, you tell him you feel great about the work you've done, about the attention your work has brought him. Tell him you want to bring the theater to a new level, but you won't be able to do so unless he can accommodate the pay increase.

Yeah! I think.

But you gotta be ready to walk. He'll know if you're not. You gotta walk in there ready to walk out.

Brian is kind of an intense guy, and I'm not sure his advice is going to work for me in the downtown theater world the way it does for him in midtown, but I appreciate the coaching.

I will approach Jim today, I decide.

My boss is in his forties. He's a great-looking hippie surfer type from Hawaii and a very brilliant, serious, and subversive director. He's an odd duck, but we're close, and he's the best boss I have ever had. He's passionate, hard working, respectful, and incredibly intelligent. He's green-lit every project I have conceived of since I started working for him: over forty concerts, a dozen theatrical productions, and a dance festival of over fifteen choreographers. If I'm into a project, I can count on his financial support and on his guidance. Because of Jim, I have my own office, my own staff of interns, and access to some of the most brilliant designers in downtown theater.

I am responsible for nearly everything: production, general management, the business management, marketing and publicity, the office management, fundraising. I am the only paid employee besides the technical director. I get about a hundred phone calls a day. I write contracts, I make deposits, I stroke egos. I work twelve-hour days at least six days a week, and I don't take vacations.

And now it's time to go for it. I walk into Jim's office where he's strumming on his ukulele. I ask him if we can talk, if I can close the door.

We are working on the rambunctious *Benten Kozo* (a production for which we win an Obie), a Kabuki play starring twenty-seven actors in their twenties. He puts down his instrument, and I shut the door to the rest of the building, which is brimming with young actors, designers, and techies. I tell him that in June it will be one year we've worked together. I tell him I'm proud of all that I've achieved with him, through him.

I am beginning to feel nervous. I felt sure with Brian, but not so sure any more.

I tell him I need a raise to continue, or else I will have to give him notice. I am so uncomfortable. He doesn't seem to be. He asks how much. I say I want to make $900 a week. (It's more than I was planning to ask, but I figured it gave me some bargaining room.)

"That's a lot of money," he says.

"I know," I say.

He says he has to check to see what other people in my position make.

I tell him I already checked, and they make much more.

He says, "But they're all in their forties."

I say, "But that's their fault."

He smiles. He says our annual budget can't sustain that kind of salary.

I say I realize he might have to take extra measures to keep me, and that it is up to him to decide if he wants to do that, because I can't sit here and convince him of my worth.

I say, "Either you know it and you'll figure out a way, or you don't know it and I should move on."

I have no idea where the confidence is coming from.

He says he has to call the accountant, and I leave his office.

I am a nervous wreck, but I keep busy and field phone calls. He comes into my office.

"The accountant," he says, "recommends two conditions."

"OK," I say.

"One is that you can't ask for more than a ten percent raise next year."

"Fine," I say.

"And two is that you have to agree to work here for two more years."

"Fine," I say.

It can't get any better than this.

Things do get better. Every show we touch becomes successful, and the work itself becomes more interesting and more challenging as time goes on. With my raise, I can afford to move into a lovely, spacious apartment in Brooklyn with a big garden in the back.

It is a special moment for me. I look around me, around my office, around my new apartment, and I see success everywhere. I have done what I set out to do. I don't know that I ever really thought this was possible for me—but look, I try to say to myself, see it is, I did it.

See? Come on. Look.

So it's strange, perhaps six months later, to be carting my belongings from my office back to Brooklyn, to be packing for a cross-country adventure.

I kept receiving signs telling me I had other work to do. It was as if success had made a lot of noise in my head go away about being successful. I wasn't screeching at myself to make more and more. I wasn't basking in the public attention I was receiving or gloating through the streets of Tribeca. No, all of a sudden, it seemed, things just got really quiet in my head. I longed for a new direction, a new devotion. And then the signs emerged.

The detour, my detour, lay ahead.

I'm on the subway, and I see this poster. It shows a woman in a business suit with the slogan "For People with Mental Illness, Treatment Is Working" across her chest. My jaw drops and my eyes tear.

I can't believe it. It's so positive, it's so true. It's me. Treatment Is Working—what a slogan. It says that treatment works and that mentally ill people are successful in the workplace and that working is therapeutic ALL AT THE SAME TIME. In one fell swoop, it works to kill stigma and it encourages people to get help and it's congratulations to those of us out there in the workplace. Who are these geniuses, I wonder—these courageous angels?

I have never seen anything like it in my whole life.

And the posters are everywhere. So in the morning as I go to the Flea and in the evenings when I return home, I see those posters, and every day I thank God that someone is out there working on this stuff. I begin to wonder why I'm not. There's so much to be done.

I have this idea. I want to find other bipolar people like me and interview them. I want them to be about my age, and ambitious and fun. I want to demonstrate how it feels to be young and bipolar, and I want to show that people survive this illness and live full lives. I want to figure out what worked in people who are success cases, and shift people's focus away from all the media attention on destructive and violent cases. I know there's a lot of drama in people gone wrong, but there's so much magic in people gone right. I want to collect people like me and reveal them to the world.

Look at us.

Look hard.

We're not who you thought we were.

And we're everywhere.

I want to produce a new image for bipolar people. I want to present new voices of bipolar people. I want this information to be available for every kid and every kid's family who goes through what my family and I went through. I want this project to encourage other young bipolar people to talk about what they've been through. I want to provide a bunch of road maps.

There's nothing out there exactly like this, I think, and I'm the person to do it, and now is the time.

I move about my life with a weight in my chest for a while, because I know I have to do this, and I know I'm creating a tremendous upheaval for myself. But I'm staying true. I'm thinking about the universe constantly; how it provides, how it communicates, how it directs. I'm preoccupied with these ideas, my brain racing, persistently creating a minireligion based on risk taking and soul searching.

And when I need encouragement, another sign intervenes.

The *NYPress,* an alternative weekly newspaper in New York, comes out with it's "Best Of" issue once a year. Of the hundreds of listings, I spot this one:

BEST SCARY SUBWAY AD

"For People with Mental Illness,
Treatment Is Working"

Crazy Train. It's the kind of bland subway advertisement you wouldn't look at twice if you didn't read the logo in the corner. It's just a picture of a well-dressed middle-aged woman in an office, smiling pleasantly at the camera. Until you read the logo, it could easily be an ad for a law firm or a job placement agency. But there it is, "For People with Mental Illness . . ." With that, everything's turned on its head. Take a look at that picture again—suddenly the pleasant smile on the woman's face has become a pained grimace, stretched tight across a skull already at the point of bursting with homicidal fantasies. Her hands, at first just clasped together calmly in her lap, become claws, clamped together in a vain attempt to keep them from slashing out at the cameraman, or her own eyes. We see a lot of crazy people on the streets, on the elevator and in the office. We know what they look like. We know what they're up to—what they're planning and what they're capable of—and we'll tell you this: It's no good. The pleasant office she's sitting in in that picture? We bet within a week the walls are smeared and splattered with buckets of her fellow employees' blood, and riddled with bullet holes after she's gone marching through the halls with an arsenal of high-powered weapons strapped to her body. "Treatment Works"; yeah, sure, in some cases—but just to be on the safe side, especially given recent events across the country, just keep them the hell away from us, OK?

I don't think I have ever seen such a malevolent example of stigma, and because it attacks the very poster campaign that so greatly impacted my life, it seems particularly virulent.

Vicious vicious vicious vicious.

Evidence of a clear and present enemy.

Fuel.

I write a letter:

Dear Fuckballs:

Fuck you and fuck your politics. Fuck your sarcasm, fuck your arrogance, get a life, get a clue.

You're promoting and creating stigma. People filled with stigma kill themselves and they hurt other people.

You don't know anything. You really don't. You're careless and shallow and directed by fear monkeys.

Positive role models give sick kids a sense that they can be well. Positive role models let sick kids have big dreams for their lives and careers for when they're well. Positive role models prevent sick kids from identifying themselves as fucked permanently. Positive role models help sick people swallow the medicine they need to survive. Positive role models are so important, and nobody's putting them out there.

You blind pig, you didn't see anything when you saw that poster. You think you're so radical, you're so edgy, you're so tell-it-like-it-is.

Some people who are sick can be treated and can be healed, and some sick people, of course, can not. The woman in the poster has a treatable disorder and is contributing to society. She is treated and well. There, unfortunately, is likely no hope or help for whatever the fuck is ailing you. . . .

But I send this letter:

Dear NYPress,

I love your newspaper, I really do. I love it when you're mean and when you're funny, but I must say I was deeply offended at "Best Scary Subway Ad" in your Best Of edition. It's going to be very difficult to keep "them" away from "us." They're everywhere, especially in newspaper offices, and treatment is working: You called me "Twentysomething Dynamo" in your Best Of issue last year. For your information, I was twenty-two, and I'm bipolar.

Take it easy, Lizzie Simon.

People ask me what a producer does all the time, and what I usually say is that a producer gets all of the crap out of the way so that the artist can express him or herself in exactly the way he or she intended. Of course there's a bunch of financial and strategic stuff involved as well, but that's really what has always interested me about producing. I felt that I was protecting and enabling strong, important voices.

And here I am, after producing the work of dozens and dozens of artists—here I am self-producing, self-protecting, clearing the way, bulldozing the bullshit for myself. It feels good.

I go about setting up my trip as if it were a production.

Things to do:

1. Call Mom and Dad. Alert them. Assure them. Ask to borrow car.
2. Quit job.
3. Make sure project strategy is indeed possible.
4. Make budget.
5. Outline ideas.
6. Get a map, a cell phone.
7. Make mix tapes for car.
8. Sublet apartment.
9. Find someone bipolar in New York to interview so you can do a practice run before you go on the road.

Everything works out. My parents are cool, Jim too. He says I can come back to the theater whenever I want. I find directories of national mental health associations, and I call dozens of chapters in the south and the west. There are indeed support groups everywhere. I can visit them to find people.

And I even find subletters: Russian guys who need to be in town for just a few months to learn new computer software or something. They are so happy to find me, and I them. Whatever it takes for the advancement of global technology—that's what I always say.

And then I describe my project to a filmmaker I interned for during college. He tells me he has the perfect candidate for my mock interview.

A real head case, he says.

But he has to be successful, I say.

This guy practically runs New York, Lizzie.

Here we go! I think. Here we go.

Actually, you've met him, he says.

I remember.

There's work to do; that's all I thought. And I want to get out of town to do it; I want to go all over the country. I want to drive across country and find out we're everywhere, everywhere, in every corner and capital. I want to find sparkling little treasures of personality who harbor terrors in their bodies, who pop the pills. I want to drive back and know for the rest of my life that they are out there. I want to meet their boyfriends and wives and know that somebody loved them, somebody wasn't scared. I want to be dazzled. I want to be taken to VIP rooms and atop mountains. I want to drive up dusty roads and see a haloed figure by the barn with electric eyes and worn clothes. I want to look at him and know I am understood. I want him to look at me and trust that I will represent him with firsthand accuracy.

As I pack in my apartment I pull out a great big box from the closet that holds my journals.

I have about thirty. I start to flip though, looking forward to being way out there alone and having all of the time in the world to breeze through them.

I find a group of short stories I had written in my second grade journal. One jumps out at me.

Get Lost! The head of the herd said to Elmer.
Poor Elmer. Everybody wants him to get lost.
One day he got an idea. He would start to walk and keep walking.
So one day he did.
Finally he found another herd and they all had the same problem.
The End

It is the third sign. There is work to do in the world, sure, but there is so much work to do within me. I must have been seven years old when I wrote that, but it captures my whole thing now! That fantasy—that finding like kind is in itself the solution—that idea is still within me. My little inner Elmer, still feeling rejected, still creating opportunities to wander and find a more understanding crowd.

It occurs to me that my little experiment, my voyage, is as

personal as it gets. I've been thinking about how much it's going
to help other bipolar people, but let's get real. Secretly, this trip
comes right out of an obsession I've carried since I was tiny, from
an ultrapersonal yearning to find my herd. *That I am going to find
my herd, another herd with the same problem, and that that will provide
the happy ending.*

Tonight I enter a new passage in my journal: *I am creating this
project for the terrorized seventeen-year-old who has just been through hell
and back. She's on the precipice of the rest of her life, but she doesn't have
the faith to know it, because all she can see, all anybody is showing her,
is the dead end she feels surrounding her. I am making this journey for
her, to help her through this, the hardest time of her life.*

*She's survived mental illness and experienced a new dimension to
existence, a fourth dimension. And that fourth dimension doesn't go away
just because her dangerous episodes do. It makes her different, and difference is always a blessing and a curse.*

*Sometimes this sense is dormant, and sometimes she'll be aware of it,
aware of how it's informing her experiences, her point of view. But as
alone as she feels in this, she isn't. I'm there, and I'm making this project from there, and I'm not going to lie to her about any of it. I know
she's flipping out beneath all of the antipsychotics they've got her on. So
I'm gonna give her some honesty, and some company in the fourth dimension. I think she's worth my time, my energy, my art, and my honesty,
because I think if she breaks through she'll change the world.*

I rip it out, satisfied.

I fold it up and stick it in my wallet for the future.

I am predicting already that a dark moment will come when
I can't remember how or why I put myself right in it.

Right in it.

part
3

I'm waiting for Nicholas Berenson at Pete's Tavern, 18th and Irving.

I'm annoyed.

I rushed to get out of work to make it up here, and he's late.

Nick will be my first interview. According to my sources, he is a thirty-two-year-old multimillionaire mover and shaker. He used to own a film company and now he owns a biotech company. He apparently comes from incredible wealth.

It's late September. The leaves are changing. New Yorkers are beginning to bundle up.

This is a rehearsal, I think nervously. It doesn't really count.

When he finally arrives, he is fifteen minutes late and wearing red tinted sunglasses and a business suit. I see him first, crossing the street to meet me.

I take in a long look. I can't read him at all, not in the first instance I see him approaching, not during the entire time we talk.

Pete's is an old historic tavern where O'Henry was supposed to have hung out. It's warm enough to sit outside, so we do.

Things are edgy at first. To begin with, Nicholas doesn't remember me, but I met him a couple of years ago through Kevin, a young independent filmmaker for whom I interned my junior year in college.

1997: Kevin took me to party at Nicholas's house. I was Kevin's only intern, and my job description blurred and spread into a bizarre full-time position with equal parts assistant, therapist, and kid sister expectations. All I had heard about Nicholas was that he owned a film company and that he was our best chance at getting the film financed. *Heroin and Hashish,* Kevin's project, was about these college students who get really into— yes, you guessed it—heroin and hashish. Kevin, who had always been more interested in people who do drugs than in doing drugs himself, had taken to making absinthe for gifts. So when he was invited to Nicholas's party he brought a bottle and invited me to come. It was sort of a big deal, Kevin and Katie, the producer, letting me hang out with them. I was very excited.

Katie knew Nicholas through her best friend, also named Katie, who was dating Nicholas. So when Kevin and the two Katies talked about Nicholas, I conjured up all sorts of glamorous fantasies about this young and dashing film producer. I couldn't believe I was going to actually meet him.

There I was, gawky and bedazzled. It was a fancy apartment in a fancy building, and they were each sort of fancy and sarcastic, talking and doing drugs and being very loud, and Nicholas's girlfriend Katie was this beautiful girl who glowed. I definitely felt like the outsider in the group, and I couldn't muster anything clever to say. It was a small party, not many more than half a dozen people there. Nicholas was really overwhelming, wrestling with Kevin, racing about the apartment. I don't remember much except that he scared me. And that I was attracted to him.

Nicholas remembers none of this. He tells me his memory's bad, that I look familiar but he doesn't know from where. And he is surprised when I tell him that I am bipolar, even though we just talked about it the other day when we were setting up this meeting.

He is also a little obsessive about how we are going to do this. Is he just supposed to talk, or am I going to ask pointed questions?

I tell him I have questions but that he can talk about anything. I try to keep things as relaxed as possible.

He doesn't.

"Well look: I don't take my meds, OK? First things first! I don't believe in it!"

I want to say, you know, you have to take your medicine, and if you don't you're really gonna fuck shit up. But instead I go into, "I'm not judging you," blah blah blah.

But he is scaring me, intimidating me, making the words tumble chunky out of my mouth, making my heart prepare for attack.

"All right," he growls, "I'm going to start with my childhood, and then I'll tell you how I was diagnosed with bipolar disorder. All right! Childhood! I was a really isolated kid. Really shy, antisocial. My friends went to public school, but I went to private school and I decided in some sort of pledge of loyalty to my public school friends that I wasn't gonna make any friends at my private school. I always felt smarter than everybody else and I always had dark nihilistic thoughts."

At Dartmouth, he says, "It got worse but I got better. I got confident."

After college he had a series of jobs ranging from carpentry work to running a newspaper his father owned in Arizona to technology work in Eastern Europe.

"I spent seven years out there," he says, "and then I got back to the States and started a film company."

He wants to explain how it is that he was diagnosed with bipolar disorder. He knows that's what I want to hear, and he wants to tell it, but he's getting frustrated. He isn't sure when the mania started. The moment isn't clear.

"We never know exactly when these things begin," I say, because it's true that we don't, and Nicholas seems bothered by his incapacity to tell a straight account.

"Yeah, I don't know when it started exactly," he says, "but I know I blew through a quarter of a million dollars in a few months. You know, manic people spend money."

Nicholas moved into a $6 thousand per month apartment. He met a seventeen-year-old lesbian girl who was handing flyers out on the street in Union Square and convinced her to be his personal assistant.

"She worshipped Zena," he says to me, in explanation of things. He paid her $1 thousand a week.

He let all kinds of weird people into his life. There was a party every night at his place. He was hypersexual and did tons of drugs. He met a homeless guy playing in the subway and let him move into his apartment, and he bought him a $2 thousand watch.

"I thought I was creating an empire," he says. "But I basically sat around in my boxers barking orders at a seventeen-year-old."

His best friends all phased out of his life, and so did his business associates. He began to carry a knife in his pocket at all times; he thought he might have to kill somebody. He never changed his shoes.

Things erupted when he decided to rent a house on Mustique island for $50 thousand. All of his friends came, and some new potential business associates: high-powered millionaire types.

Things were wrong. He was running around the small island carelessly in a manic fury. His guests started slipping Valium into his drinks to calm him, to get him to sleep. He broke his ankle. He wrecked a car.

"I don't remember most of it," he tells me.

The day after he got back to New York, he went to an intimate Oscar party at his buddy Gary's house. "There are about twenty people there," he tells me, "two of whom are Kate Moss and Leonardo DiCaprio." Nicholas starts a fight with Leonardo

DiCaprio and wrestles him to the ground before being forced to leave.

"I was out of it," Nicholas says, "but that kid's a prick."

Nicholas had been manic like this for months, and everybody in his life, old friends and new, were aware of it. Nobody knew what to do with him.

Nicholas tells me he began to despair. "I gave up," he says, "I was like Fuck you. Fuck all of you." His parents told him they'd like him to go to the hospital for a day to get some testing. He said, "Fine." He got to the hospital and his old friend Kyle was there, along with his parents and an employee of his father's company, named Albert.

Nicholas starts to wonder why Kyle's there.

He asks if he can speak to Kyle alone in a room, please.

Everybody says, "Sure."

Nicholas asks him what's going on.

"They just want to run some tests," Kyle says.

"Well," Nicholas says, "I've got a big fat joint in my pocket, and I'm going into the hospital baked."

"All right," says Kyle.

Albert accompanies the two for a walk.

Nicholas lights the joint, and they walk toward Central Park.

But Nick knows what's going on.

They are all trying to trap him.

They think they've got him.

He spots a police car near the park.

Nicholas tries to wave the joint at them, hoping to instigate something, hoping to get arrested.

No response.

Nicholas gives the cops the finger. He shows them the joint.

But it doesn't work. The cops ignore him, and Nicholas is stuck, walking with Kyle and Albert closely on both sides. They are holding his arms.

Nicholas stops them.

"Kyle," he says, "I have a huge bag of pot in my pocket. Let me give it to you before I admit myself. They're never going to let me take it in, Kyle; it'll just go to waste, and it's really good stuff."

That seems reasonable. They let go of Nicholas for a second to let him find his stash.

Nicholas immediately takes off for the subway, but he isn't fast enough for Kyle, who body slams him into the wall of a building. They wrestle about for a while—"I have a little fit"—and then Albert and Kyle return Nicholas to the hospital.

Nicholas's pants are torn and his face is bleeding. His mother, who Nicholas says dressed up for the occasion, is horrified. Or at least Nicholas is horrified. Kyle's got him in a full nelson.

Don't let my parents see me like this, he thinks, and calms himself.

Kyle and Albert guide him deeper into the hospital, where a doctor tells Nicholas that they are going to put him on Haldol. Nicholas says, "Oh really? I doubt that" and tries to start another fight. There was a pile-on, he says, of seven guys. They get him onto a table, cuff his arms, strap his legs down, and have a guy holding his head. Nicholas says he was speed talking: "Oh really, you're a doctor?" things like that, a mile a minute, anything to mock the people in the hospital.

Nicholas says he continued to fight, and the doctors told him that if he didn't calm down they would have to give him a shot in the ass.

He started screaming, you can't pull my pants down.

"And the doctor was like, oh yeah, why not, and I said, cause you're gonna see my dick and you're gonna wanna suck it all day long."

The doctors and orderlies started to crack up, he says, and they let go of their tight grip of Nicholas enough so that he could begin to strangle one of the orderlies.

"Like this," he says, leaning over the table to fake strangle me.

"Then they got serious," Nicholas says, "and they shot me up with Haldol and I was out for three days. And that was my induction into the world of manic depression."

They put him into a secure room with a window. He shared a common area with a woman who threw shitty diapers at the wall, and a suicidal seventeen-year-old. Ward 8, he remembers.

They got him to do art therapy.

He asks if I would like to see his art therapy and I say I would.

"It's good," he says. "It's framable."

I just nod.

"I know; I collect art," he says.

And then Nicholas was admitted to Silver Hill, where he spent a month getting therapy and drug treatment. When he got out, he felt droopy and out of it and wanted to feel himself again, so he did "mountains of cocaine for a month."

Nicholas begins to tell me how suicidal he was, that it was like he had a noose hanging on his door. And then he tells me about his gun collection. I don't know anything about guns, so I ask him to list what he's got. They're all at his parents' house, he says, but here goes: 12-gauge shotgun, AR-15 assault rifle, a Ruger mini 14 rifle, a 30-30 Winchester, three 20-gauge shotguns, an MI short barrel, and a Taurus 9-millimeter pistol.

I ask him if he's afraid he might take a gun and shoot people randomly. He says, "Absolutely not." He would never hurt anybody.

"But Nicholas," I say, "you just finished telling me how violent you get when you're manic. Aren't you afraid you'd be out of your mind and you might do something terrible?"

"No," he says. "Everybody's afraid I'm gonna do that, but I'm not. When I got out, I had no life, I had no friends. All I did was walk around the city." He tells me how dogs and kids follow him around. "It's adults I can't stand. Their masks, how they deceive each other. I like honesty," Nicholas says, "and that's what you get from dogs and kids."

I ask Nicholas if he feels betrayed by everyone who was on Mustique with him.

"I think they're limited," he says.

I imagine Nicholas might be a good doctor. He's so smart—maybe he could advance the field of psychiatry.

"Why don't I go to med school? I don't want to help people. I don't. I think I'd be good at it. But I don't want to. I want my own little turf that is my life, and these [episodes of mania] initiated an exploration of what my turf could be. I think a lot of the things I was feeling when I was hypermanic . . . Lizzie, you say you didn't sleep for, what, a couple weeks?" He points to himself. "Six months. That will make you crazy. I didn't sleep for six months. You know, maybe two hours a night. It made me more aware, blah blah blah. It also made me delusional, and, you know, not a good way to go about personal hygiene for your mind."

Is he making sense? I can't tell.

Nick says he almost died from a near-toxic dose of antidepressants. "If I'm gonna die," he says, "I don't want to die because I'm so smothered by your medication that my heart stops beating. I want to die in a blaze of glory. The only way to describe Depakote is that it put me under water. I felt like I was submerged. No one heard me. I didn't hear them. I didn't know where I was. I was absolutely motionless and lifeless."

I ask him if he's aware that the illness gets worse with age.

"Yes," he says, simply.

"What do you think of that?" I ask.

"Don't have kids," he says. "I mean, I'm going to. But not until I find the right woman—and no woman in her right mind would marry me."

"Why?"

"Cause I'm a nut. I am a nut. A nice nut. I'm not going to hurt anybody. I mean I haven't had a real girlfriend. . . . It's much easier for me to define what I want to do alone in the world than if another person and I agreed upon a relationship. I'm a romantic. I've always wanted to feel love and fall in love—love my kids, love my wife, see the world through four eyes instead of two eyes, and just really appreciate all of the time I have here as honestly as

I can. I think I can do that. I just don't think I can do that here right now. And I don't think I can do it with just anyone. I think it's gotta be a very specific person who understands that I like myself not sedated—not necessarily manic, but I am who I am, and I don't want drugs to mask that. And that's a double-edged sword because there's that danger of going off and alienating everyone again. But I have the hindsight now where I can sort of moderate what I do, my actions and my reactions to things, and more clearly understand the boundaries between me and other people. And more clearly understand what I'm capable of doing."

"I'm a guy who likes people," he says, continuing. "I like to bond with people; I like to be around people; I like to hear what they have to say. I like to share insights. I like to understand what other people think. And it's lonely when, because of one considered debilitation, you isolate yourself from the greater part of society. And whatever anybody says, there is a stigma against crazy people. I worked in a nuthouse, St. Elizabeth's Hospital down in Washington, DC, for a year, with a public defender, helping them get out into civilization. And I felt more at home talking to the psychotic than I did talking to the lawyers. When I was there— this was 1987—I always knew that I would be there one day. I didn't know how or why, and I didn't believe it when it happened. But I knew that there was something really wrong with me."

I just nod.

"And I'm terrified. I'm terrified now about winding up a fucking homeless crazy guy. I'll admit that. I think there comes a time in everybody's life when they decide to interact with society, participate in whatever we're doing there. And I just have to figure out how to fit a square peg in a round hole and do it without shaving off too much of the part."

So I try to tell him that I'm going cross country; I'm doing this project because I want to find my herd, that I feel a pretty intense longing to be understood.

Nicholas says yeah, yeah, yeah, nodding. But it doesn't seem to be seeping in at all.

"I've got my dog," he says, cutting me off. "Honestly. My dog's the greatest dog in the world. And I've got my dog and I don't care if you or anybody else understands me. I don't need that. I've been through times when I needed that: understanding and acceptance. Remember now, I'm thirty-two, not twenty-three. And I've had years of people not understanding me, Lizzie. I'm gonna be alone when I die and when I live. Even if I get married, it's not going to change anything. There are certain rooms that are closed off to everybody else whether you want to let them in or not. They won't be able to enter appropriately, and they'll show up like a misunderstood inlaw who thinks he's coming for the right weekend when he's come for the wrong weekend. I want to have fun, and I want to get shit done. And if I meet a girl, fine, and if I don't, fine. And I'm very alone. I've always been lonely. And I can't have a girlfriend. I haven't had a real girlfriend since—for ten years."

I wonder, why does he keep bringing up the girlfriend thing?

"Have you ever been to a support group?" I ask, changing the subject.

"No, Lizzie. I don't care what other people think. I don't need to hear other people's stories. They don't mean much to me. All they mean is we share a common experience. But that common experience doesn't define a necessary outcome. They're not going to help me with what I think or what I feel. If I want a huggy kissy session I can go and get a hug from my sister or play with my dog."

The waitress passes us without stopping to get another drink order from Nicholas. He's had four black and tans since we've been here. I haven't finished one. "Now if I could only get her attention it would keep me from chopping her head off."

He continues. "Listen, I've been to AA. When I was at Silver Hill I got a lot of drug and alcohol counseling. I was lucky. My drug binge was a month. Some people do it for five years. But I did it with such intensity that it wreaked havoc. Support group's like, OK so we're all really fucked up here sitting in a cauldron of our own mess. What do we do now? Well, let's hug each other and cry a lot, and you might feel better at the end of the day, but it doesn't help you. I don't think so. I mean it might help some people like organized religion, but that's not my gig. I mean, you exist outside of me and I exist outside of you, and our experiences are very different, and we're going to go about our treatments in a very different manner and with a different attitude. And personal experience aside, I mean what do you want to get out of this? And is it helpful to share that experience with other people? Is it like a Band-Aid? Or does it help you define your root? And I don't think it helps me define my root. As a Band-Aid, sure, maybe, but it doesn't mean anything. I've always felt isolated and alone, and now I've got my badge of insanity to carry around with me that most people know about, and I don't give a fuck what they think. I can function within society a lot better than most, and I don't want people's help in doing that. So I'm not trying to be antagonistic, but like, I think my parents should go to a support group and not me."

Nicholas signals the hostess to our table. She is an older woman in her fifties with long blond frizzy hair. She sits on a stool under a tree beside the outside seating. "Vega!" Nicholas says, and she rushes over. He must come here a lot.

Nicholas looks at me and sort of gestures my way to the hostess.

"Isn't she cute?" Nicholas says. "Isn't she cute?"

"She is cute," the hostess says to him, "but you are cute, too."

"She's adorable, though," Nicholas says.

I blush and awkwardly sip my beer but miss my mouth by a few centimeters.

"How's everything else?" the hostess asks.

"Life is beautiful," Nick says.

"I'm looking for a job," the hostess says.

"You are? What do you want to do? You've got a job!"

"I can't work inside there. It's too polluted. Do you have any connections?"

"What do you want to do?"

"Coat check."

"Yeah, I do. Hold on. I don't know what his deal is. But he's opening up a restaurant downtown. Supposed to be the really new hip restaurant. Seriously."

"Give me your phone number."

"All right. Give me a pen."

"Tell him you know me for long time."

"I know. I'm gonna give you my phone number. I'm gonna call my buddy."

"Tell him she's a little bit older, but you know, she's good"

"He's totally the coolest guy in New York City, all right? So if he meets you, he'll hire you. Because you're equally cool. But I don't know what he's done. He's opening the restaurant in about three weeks. I don't know who he's hired. I don't know anything. But I will call him and I will tell him about you."

"If he needs hostess or coat check."

"I know, but it's like ultra hip, so like everything he does is designed. I don't know what he's into. And he's not managing the restaurant. He's just an internet guy; he's just investing. But if they see you, they'll be like 'that chick's cool.' You're cool, so I will do what I can."

And then they start speaking in Russian.

I leave to go the bathroom, and when I come back he's alone at the table.

He continues talking.

"When I was cooked, I would call people in California until three, I would call people in Russia, until the sun came up and then I would go to work."

I don't react.

"Look, I'm just sick and tired of being considered sick, and I think everybody's ready to get over that. I think my parents would like to beat the point into my forehead like a nail."

I ask him why he thinks they're doing that.

"Because I think they have their own issues. The longer they can manage my life, the better. I work with my dad, which makes it very difficult; I shouldn't be working with my dad. But I'll tell you the thing. I loved being crazy. I loved it, I loved every minute. Only at the end, in Mustique, where things started to fall apart. So that awakening . . . you know my best friend, Kyle, came to visit me in the hospital, like five or six days into it; very different kind of guy, married, just bought a house, but we've known each other since we were three, and I said, 'Kyle, you know, they're all telling me I was nuts for the past nine months, what the fuck? You've known me your whole life. You tell me; they may have agendas; I want to know what you think.'

"He says, 'Nick, you know why I didn't talk to you for nine months? Because you were a vile fool.'

"That's a quote."

Then Nick's friend Rick arrives out of nowhere. They begin figuring out some music industry deal. It gives me a chance to think. A chance to realize that I should take off.

As I go, the hostess sidles up to me and tells me she thinks Nicholas is really cute.

"He's special. He's a good one," she tells me. She's trying to sell him on me.

On the subway home I try to convince myself that I will never see him again.

He's definitely not right for my project.

He's negative.

He doesn't take his meds.

He drinks too much.

And I don't care how much money he's got or what industries he reigns as king; he is not successful according to my standards.

But that night while I sleep, Nicholas appears in every dream.

Wild vivid dreams about coming together at the end of the world.

Nobody knows why certain rocks become magnetized and others don't. I read a book about it: *Driven Force* by Robert Livingston. Magnetic movement happens because elements brewing deep beneath the earth respond to certain inner magnetic systems of certain substances. Magnetism is earthly driven, while all other movement depends on direct touch.

Of course, not everything is highly magnetic. Some rocks are; some rocks are not. But our brains are. Our brains are electromagnetic systems.

A lodestone is a variety of magnetite that shows polarity and acts like a magnet when freely suspended. The word for lodestone in Chinese is *tzhu shih,* which means "loving stone." Scientists have scratched their heads for centuries as to why lodestones are magnetized. They think it might have something to do with material that is struck at random by bolts of lighting—*changed in a flash from the sky, by chance, from rocks to loving stones.*

It's the morning after my last night of work at the theater.

I'm anxious because I don't have a theater to carry on my back any more, and to my surprise I don't quite know how to move without its weight.

I wake up early.

My apartment is a mess. I have weeks of laundry to do and a mountain of dishes in the sink. There are dust balls the size of golf balls in every corner.

But I can't seem to do anything.

I don't really want to sit around.

I sort of have a cold, so I can't go to yoga, and my friends are busy or sleeping.

And I don't really want to be around people because I feel edgy, and I don't think anybody could understand where I am.

I'm thinking about all the stuff I need to do before my trip, but it's all stuff I have to wait for a weekday to do. So I pull some stuff out of the fridge to make an omelet and the idea occurs to me to call Nicholas.

To see if I can see some of those pictures he drew in art therapy when he was hospitalized.

So I call him and at first he seems really happy to hear from me, but then he's edgy and I feel like a pain in the ass. He says I can come over to see the pictures, but I have to come immediately.

I'm in my pjs.

I haven't showered for a few days. I am still crusty from my going-away party two nights before, from Garrett and Genevieve going nuts on my hair with gel.

But I decide it's OK if I'm a little grody around Nicholas.

I put on a pair of jeans and go.

I get on the train, and I get to Nicholas's house, and the doorman calls up and I hear Nicholas barking at the doorman through the phone. The doorman mumbles "asshole" after he sets the phone down, and he points me in the direction of the elevators. I go to the top floor and walk up an extra flight. Nicholas has the penthouse apartment, and the door's open, and the music's blasting, and it's just after noon, and Nicholas has a Guinness, and the place reeks of booze and smoke.

Albert is there, and he has a black eye. He acts like a guard dog, hovering around Nicholas, ready to growl.

I wonder how I'm supposed to communicate with Nicholas with Albert there.

Nick's place is humongous. It's in the shape of a half pyramid, and the slanted wall is entirely glass. On that day the sky is blue and clear. Nicholas and Albert are sitting on leather couches staring tensely at each other.

"Lizzie's a writer," Nicholas says. "She's writing about me."

Albert's not happy. I stay quiet.

Art hangs on the wall—fancy art, boy art (messy, violent art). He tells me the names of the artists. I've heard of one. Condo. He's got two. And Dali, yes, he's got a Dali. An ex-girlfriend gave it to him.

"Can I see the stuff you did in the hospital?"

He ignores me.

I'm impressed. This is it; this is what you imagine when you imagine a young millionaire in Manhattan. This apartment.

The pyramid glass side has iron beams, which are rigged for climbing.

"You climb?" I ask.

"Yes," he says.

The room has the worst aura. Maybe he wants me to leave.

"Can I get a glass of water?"

Sure, he says. I go to the kitchen, find a glass, and fill it with water and ice. There's nothing in the fridge or freezer but booze and a can of open sardines.

Nicholas lets me know that something happened last night.

"You tell her the story, Albert," he says.

"Ah," Albert starts with a thick Polish accent. "Nicholas was, he was, well, you might know more about this stuff, he was very sped up and manic, and I tried to take care of him, and we began to fight, and he punched me."

Nicholas looks at me for my reaction.

"Oh," is all I say.

Albert leaves the apartment to get Nicholas's car.

Nick and I go alone to the roof of his building to see the view.

It's a clear day. I can see for miles.

We sit on lawn chairs and gaze out.

"Look," he says, "I know that I'm out of control. And I know I need help. And I'm gonna cut the bullshit and get help. And I'm so glad you're here to witness this, Lizzie, because honestly, today is the first real day of my life"

I want to believe I am witnessing a major turning point in someone's life. That point where things are so bad that they decide to commit themselves completely to recovery. I make sure to look him straight in the eye.

He lights a joint and passes it to me.

I puff. Normally I'd be at work on a day like today. Not any more. This is my job now, right? Doing bipolar research.

We look at each other for a little while.

"This is none of my business," I say, "but Nicholas, you're not going to be able to have a real life until you take your medicine."

"I know," he says.

His face is precious and innocent for a moment. It is so quiet and still up here. He's really not an asshole at all, I think. He's a scared little boy.

"It makes me feel like I'm dead," he says.

"Find a better medicine," I say. "Ask your doctor. Do you like your doctor?"

"Yeah, I have the coolest doctor."

"Talk to him, then. There's something out there that'll work."

He stares into space. "You like lithium?" he asks skeptically.

"Yeah, a lot."

"It doesn't slow you down?"

"No, not at all. I'm taking over the universe," I say, and smile.

"I would be too," he says, not really believing it.

"Of course you would be," I say.

"I bet bipolar people would run the world if they were treated," he says.

"I bet the treated ones already do," I say.

He grins. He's a little boy. A sweet, gentle boy, who does not deserve this mess.

"I'm calling my doctor," he says. And he does. He leaves a message that he'd like to go back on meds and could he please call back.

Nicholas lets me talk right to him, right into his head and heart and soul. He just opens up and says come right in, and we talk about it: the illness, the terror, the world, the alienation, the beauty and the ugliness of all of it. And he's the first, the first I've ever met who has talked to me in this way. And I'm supposed to be his angel right now, but I have never felt so damn fucking understood. My heart is welling up, and somewhere inside of me I have been woken up and been told a little boy has come over and he is so sorry I've been left alone for so long but he is here and he understands everything and he will hold my hand forever if I want because he loves me very very very much.

We're on the roof, looking over lower Manhattan on wooden lawn chairs. We're not touching or anything. Nothing sexual is passing between us. But there is a thickness in the air.

I look at him and I think, there's somebody who will recover if only somebody will stick by him through it all. I decide to be that person.

He just needs a clean house, and some groceries, and a few weeks of regular sleep, and his meds—he needs to be taking his meds absolutely—and some real friends, and some information for his loved ones. And he needs to lay off the booze and mellow out and stop trying to live the rock and roll life and start just being the human being he is, and start writing in a journal, and reading good books and feeling the warmth and power of my friendship. . . .

I look at him and see him in an imaginary few months from now: cleaned up, in control, brilliant, loving, adorable.

My perfect partner, because at the end of the day, Nicholas understands where I have been.

I look at Nicholas and I see somebody to save, a project worthy of my devotion.

We step into our own fourth dimensions—and look, we have company: each other.

We discuss our brains as if they were our farms. Over there that's the where the pigs live, and I have to do this to maintain the pigs, and that stretch of land, that's where corn might grow. We imagine that normal brains are like a flat field and our bipolar brains have every kind of possible landscaping known to Mother Nature.

We go down into his apartment, and he rigs me up so I can climb everywhere. I step awkwardly into the harness and start climbing up the steel beams.

"Jump off," he says.

I do. He's holding me up when I swing. I am only aware of how great I feel at that moment, in that moment.

Which is a brief moment: The phone rings, and he lets me down. It's his doctor. Nicholas starts to tell him what's going on. His voice begins to break.

"I want to go back on meds," he says, and begins to cry.

I want to wrap him up inside of me. I sit on the arm of his chair and put my hand on his back, to let him know I'm not afraid of any of this. When he gets off the phone he gets up brusquely and goes to the bathroom. He seems together when he gets out. He looks me straight in the eye and says thanks.

It feels so right to do something for someone, something you wish someone had done for you. So right it's completely intoxicating.

Something tremendous has happened between us. I am sure of that, and I am sure he feels the same way. And I can see so clearly that this phase he is in will pass. He is so ripe for recovery. Soon we will remember this meeting as if it were another world.

When he is well, this will all seem a dream.

Albert comes back with his girlfriend, Puscha, and the car and they are all going away for the weekend to Nicholas's cabin in Schroon Lake, New York.

"What are you doing?" he says.

I shrug.

"Come," he says.

I think for a second or two.

"OK," I say.

Detour.

We're in the car. Albert and Puscha are in the front seat. What must they think of me? I have no idea. Does Nicholas drag girls up to Schroon Lake all the time? They don't seem to care. They are simply preoccupied with him. He's snuck some beers in his pants and jacket and is about to open one when Puscha rips it from his hand. The two begin a screaming match. I can't believe her behavior. I mean, the guy's trying to get through the day. His brain is probably all over the place. Let him have a beer.

"He's self-medicating," I say, and Albert laughs.

"That's a good one—self-medicating," he says.

What an asshole, I think.

Nick and Albert tell me the story of their meeting in Yugoslavia, how they became associates, how Nick's dad brought Albert and Puscha to the States, how he set them up with jobs, an apartment, a Lexus.

"Wow," I say. When I ask what Albert does for the company, I get a very vague answer.

Nick announces that he wants to stop at his parents' house before we get to the cabin. It's sort of on the way. He wants to pick up his dog, Tank; but he doesn't want to see his parents, so he asks Albert to park outside the estate and wait for him to sneak in, grab the dog, and sneak out.

Albert says that this is ridiculous, that he won't do it, it's disrespectful.

Nick and Albert begin screaming at each other, and Puscha jumps in to make the noise unbearable. What the hell are they fighting about again? Oh yeah, Nick wants to sneak in and steal his dog for the night, and Albert won't be an accomplice.

"Nick," I say softly, tugging on his shirt.

"What," he says, totally switched off, calm, sweet.

"Why can't you just see your parents, say hello, get the dog, and we'll go?"

He grunts. "It's too . . . you don't understand; I can't . . . I'm in no state to see my parents."

"Why not?" I say. "You're fine; you're just a little drunk. But you're not acting weird. You're not crazy. You're not having an episode."

"Sweetie, I can't," he says.

"Sure you can," I say. "You're fine; you're just starting over. They'll understand, won't they? Just be honest. Tell them you're a mess, you're gonna get better, you're gonna start your medicine. Just tell them it's all gonna be better."

We get to Chez Berenson. It's a huge gorgeous house on acres of land. Pool, tennis courts, the works.

Mr. Berenson has just pulled into the driveway when we arrive. Albert and Puscha get excited. He just bought the new blah blah blah model number blah blah blah. It's some ultra-fancy car. They are like groupies just outside Jon Bon Jovi's dressing room door. In a tizzy.

Nick bolts from the car into the house, and Albert and Puscha rush to Mr. Berenson.

Puscha leans in immediately: "Let me help you with your things."

Mr. Berenson barks her out of his way.

Puscha's wheels turn. "Nick's drunk," she says. "I wanted to warn you. He's completely out of control. He punched Albert last night."

Albert stands there with his black eye.

"I'm sorry, Albert," Mr. Berenson says, and he walks towards the house. He sees me.

I freeze. "I'm Nick's friend Lizzie," I say warmly. I want to convey that I am completely normal. I wish I had showered some time in the past two days and that I wasn't wearing the top that I slept in last night.

Mr. Berenson smiles and says hello wearily.

We go into the kitchen, where Nick's mom is waiting. Albert and Puscha greet her with hugs and kisses. Nick's mom is a pretty blond in her sixties.

"What is going on with Nicholas?" she asks. "Is he OK?"

"He was out of control. He punched me last night," Albert says.

Nick's mom closes her eyes.

"But he seems to be better this morning," he says.

"This is Lizzie," Puscha said. "She's Nick's new friend. She's bipolar too. She's coming with us to Schroon Lake. They met this morning."

"No, that's not true," I say, and I smile graciously. Puscha's a jackass.

"I hope you can handle Nicholas," she says.

"No, she likes them wild," Puscha says, smiling.

I am going to kill her.

"No, I don't," I say, sticking up for myself. "And Nick's fine," I add. "He's not manic or anything, just a little drunk. He called his doctor. He's starting over. He's going to take his medicine."

"You're bipolar?" his mom asks incredulously, and so begins a fifteen-minute conversation, very intense for two people who have never met before.

In the car I figured Nicholas had evil, uncaring parents. It's not true at all. They are both warm, sensitive and intelligent. Lost, confused, misdirected, perhaps—but that's decent. How is any-body supposed to know how to handle their mentally ill child? It seems clear to me: Nick just needs to start over. Leave this shit behind.

He needs to start getting the fact that his family loves him and wants to help him. And stop pushing them away.

Hey there . . .

I remember that as a child, I was unusually preoccupied with fears of being kidnapped. It didn't help that my older brother, Aaron, would tell me tales of The Black Van roaming our neigh-borhood capturing small children. "The Black Van, Lizzie; you haven't seen it? It's black, and the windows are dark, and it goes really fast. They just slide the side door open and bam! they grab ya."

I was a very small child. Loud, but small. People in school called me Little Lizzie (and people at the theater called me Ethel Merman). I knew I was easy to grab. When nobody was around, I practiced screaming.

Aaron walked me to school in the mornings. He was three grades higher than me, and I believed every word he ever told me. But he spent a lot of time tricking and torturing me. I was already a neurotic kid, but Aaron enjoyed giving me a few more things to let my little head nibble on. There was, for instance, a walkway that he called the Gay Bridge. If you walked under it, you'd be gay, which was at the time the weirdest freak fate possi-ble to us kids. So I tried avoiding it, but Aaron would sort of throw me under it from time to time, especially when his friends were around. Then I would have to invent all sorts of theoretical hexes to unGay myself. Occasionally he would conspire with me and not against me. Like we used to give this chubby kid Sammy a dime to dance to "Men at Work." It was great fun.

Aaron was the happiest person I knew. I think he still is. He had his backyard and his friends, and he had baseball. Aaron played a lot of baseball, a lot of homerun derby. I always got to pitch homerun derby. And get my face nailed with tennis balls. Most of the situations Aaron put me in resulted in bruising. He loved WWF and would want to practice moves on me. My nose bled at least a hundred times, and I would tell on him, but he and my mother had some sort of silent agreement that I shouldn't win our fights, and I didn't dare go to my father. You just never bothered dad.

But June took my side. She was our housekeeper, and she protected me. June was about five feet tall, but she knew karate. "Leave your sister alone!" she'd say and toss my brother to the ground. Aaron thought she was pretty cool too.

So anyway, Aaron would always talk about The Black Van, and I had pretty much accepted my probable fate as a kidnappee. I would bug my mom about it all the time:

"What's the plan if I get kidnapped, mom?"

"Don't worry about it," she'd say. "You're not gonna get kidnapped. We're not rich enough."

"But The Black Van, Mom—it's in our neighborhood. What would you and Daddy do?"

"Lizzie," she'd assure me, "it's not gonna happen."

"But Mom," I'd nag, "what would you do if someone wanted a large ransom for me?"

"Daddy would pay it," she'd say.

"MOM! But what if it were a million dollars, Mom? YOU AND DADDY DON'T HAVE A MILLION DOLLARS!"

"Don't worry about it," she would say.

"NO!" I wanted to discuss these things. "What would you do, Mom?"

She would sigh and tell me that they would figure out a way, take a big loan from the bank. She promised that all of my aunts and uncles and grandparents would sell their homes and their summer homes just to get me back.

It sort of blew me away. I believed her; this impressed me,

but I knew that no one in my family would ever feel the same way about me, that their sacrifice would make them resent me, and that I would feel guilty for the rest of my life. I would have drained my whole family.

The little thing in me knew somehow that it would all happen, that one day I'd be stolen, and that getting me back would drain everybody around me and give me a guilt I'd never completely shrug.

I haven't really spent any time at home since I went crazy.

Schroon Lake is a good time. A very good time. We fish, we canoe, we hike through the woods. We make a bonfire and cook kielbasa and potatoes.

We talk, the two of us, and talk and talk and talk and talk.

From time to time I think, nobody knows where I am.

I even warm up to Puscha. She was just suspicious of me at first; I suppose it's understandable.

By the fire that Saturday night, Puscha and Albert are in their little world and we are in ours. My head is in Nick's lap, and I am gazing up to his blue blue eyes, and the Flea and my book project couldn't be farther away. Nicholas is speaking backward to me, in full fluid sentences. My mind is racing to keep up with him. "Ym eman si Kcin. Ruoy eman si Eizzil," he'd rattle off.

"My name is Nick, your name is Lizzie!" I figure out eventually.

"Ouy era cigam ot em," he says.

"Huh?"

"Ouy era cigam ot em."

"You . . . are . . . cigam . . . magic . . . to me." I smile at him. He gets serious. "You are magic to me too," I say lightly. I'm a little drunk.

"Reven evael em," he says.

Never . . . leave . . . "Okay," I say. "Except I have to leave for my project on Tuesday; is that OK?"

"This Tuesday?" he asks.

"Yeah."

"How long will you be gone for?"

"I don't know."

"What do you mean—you don't know?"

"I don't know. However long it takes me to find people for my project. At least a month, not longer than two months."

Nick gets quiet. We're just sitting there.

"I evol uoy," he says and I look at him really hard. Did he

really say that? Could he mean that? He doesn't even know me.

"Let's go for a walk," he says, and we go down to the docks. Five seconds later I'm naked, naked on a dock under the light of a half moon on a still lake in the middle of nowhere. And I want to run as fast as Nicholas, I want to let him do whatever he wants.

I tnaw su ot ecneirepxe modeerf rehtegot.

The next morning, Nick drives me into town and takes me out to breakfast. I show him some of my writing. We talk in detail about my book project. Nick delivers a dizzying pep talk.

You are our voice, Lizzie.

You are going to change the world for us, Lizzie.

You are a force of nature.

You are an angel.

You are a genius, Lizzie: a daredevil, a poet, a goddess.

You are magic; you are beautiful, Lizzie. You are touched by something from another world.

Don't fuck this up, Lizzie. This is so important to us, sweetie. Don't let us down.

He thinks he is being supportive.

When we get back to his house, we lie on the dock for a while. He asks me about my parents, my brothers. I tell him that my older brother is a broker, and Nick begins telling me he is having a hard time with his own broker, who is also one of his best friends, Gary Angelone.

"He's a broker to the stars. That's how I know most of the people I know in New York, through Gary. He has another bipolar friend, Joe, who's like the top agent at William Morris, the top guy. None of us take our meds. Gary always tells me, 'Don't take that shit: You, me and Joe, we're different.'"

"Do you believe that?" I ask.

"I don't know," he says.

He tells me he'd like to give my brother a call.

(Over the next few weeks, Nick transfers large loads of money to my brother, the amount of which my brother never reveals.)

Magnetic: 4. Possessing personal attractiveness.

Oh, did I mention it? He's hot, he's fucking hot. He looks like Sean fucking Penn. He just looks at you and you get dizzy, and my God he's got these eyes and this smirk, and a swagger, he swaggers! He barks! And he's electric when he's telling a story and he's hot, literally hot, steamy: you know, approaching him is approaching heat. He makes you feel as if you're Miss America, and you're looking at him, and he's JUST SO SEXY everybody else disappears.

We spend Sunday night at Nick's parents' house. On the drive there we listen to a Tornado CD. Nick's roommate, though seldom around, is Rick Morehouse, the group's lead singer. (I have never heard of them, but it turns out, of course, that my older brother is a huge fan. Later Nick invites him up from Boston for a show, takes him backstage, the whole nine.)

Nick's mom finds me a change of clothes, and I shower and clean up and feel good. The Berensons are wonderful people; we get along very easily.

But Nick is a mess. Being home seems to deplete his energies. He is pained by even the most innocent questions his parents pose concerning his activities, his whereabouts, his companions. He starts drinking the second we get to the house, and by the time dinner is over he is slurring his words and wandering around.

But I forgive his behavior.

The things he understands.

About loneliness. Nick brings me to the porch. It is pouring outside, and I sit in his lap facing him, and he tells me how alone he is, and I know what he means, and then he seems angry, suddenly, and he tells me he's been this alone and misunderstood for ten years longer than me.

He's like the potatoes we cooked in the fire. They look like balls of charred matter, but inside there's still plenty of stuff, and if you add butter and salt it's a dream to eat.

But Nicholas is pretty charred. He drinks so much tonight, maybe a bottle of wine and a few glasses of whiskey in four hours time.

When everybody goes to bed, we go to the living room to watch movies. He starts to scare me. His eyes are droopy, and he starts to say some weird things: things I can't understand. He is suddenly angry at me, telling me I am going to leave him. I don't know what he is talking about. I have never felt so in love with anybody in my whole life. I am totally committed.

But I just don't feel safe any more. He asks me if I love him, and I say I don't know. He is so drunk and his dick is limp and I am just scared of him. He drank whatever magic he has with me. And I don't want to sleep on the couch with him. This house has seven bedrooms; why are we on this couch? I wake him up and tell him I am going upstairs to sleep in his room.

I do love him. I lied. I ache for him the second he starts to drink too much, because he goes away and I want him near.

I go upstairs and find Nick's bedroom and climb into his bed. A few hours later, Nick storms into his room and wakes me. It is the middle of the night.

"WHAT ARE YOU DOING?! WHERE HAVE YOU BEEN?!" he roars.

My mind starts to race. He seems more angry at me than anybody has ever been before.

"I'm sorry. I woke you, Nick; I told you I was going upstairs to sleep."

"I NEVER THOUGHT YOU WOULD LEAVE ME!" he says in a vicious tone, and then he gets into bed. I think he is going to attack me, but he just passes out.

We leave early the next morning. Mr. Berenson drives Nick and me into the city. Nick is complaining about what an asshole Albert is and how much he hates working with him.

"Nick, he's your friend."

"No, he's not."

"Well, he's the best friend you've got."

"I don't have any friends. I don't want any friends."

"I'm your friend," I peep in from the back seat. Nick reaches his hand back and I hold it.

It's very tense in the car.

Mr. Berenson asks me about my career as a producer and then about my project.

"So you're an expert, ah?"

Fuck. He's testing me. "No, not at all. I'm just kind of a expert in me."

"How old are you?"

"I'm twenty-three."

"Oh, Nick—she's a baby." he says. What's that supposed to mean?

"And where did you sleep last night?" he asks. None of your fucking business.

"In Nick's bed," I say confidently, and everybody shuts up.

We get into the city and say good-bye. Nick's going to work. He says he'll call me later. I am completely exhausted. I go home and sleep all day long.

That night is my last night in town. I meet Nick and his friend Jenny at the Mercury Lounge. One of Nick's friends is in a band playing there. I arrive, and Nick and Jenny are sitting at a table in the front. I have brought something for Nick, a silver jewelry box that looks like a treasure chest. It was a bat mitzvah gift from years ago, not exactly fitting for Nick, but I had an overwhelming urge to give him something—something tangible. I hand it to him, and his eyes start to well up with tears, and he excuses himself and leaves the table.

"I've never seen him like this," Jenny says. "He's totally head over heels."

Jenny is very pretty and warm. She knows Nick through Rick. We bond immediately. Nick is gone only for a minute, but in that time she assures me that I have nothing to worry about.

"In terms of leaving for two months, Nick has no other romantic situations going on. He's very loyal; he'll be in love with you for life; he's just that kind of guy."

Later, when we are alone, Nick asks me over and over again if I love him, why I love him, am I sure I love him, will I love him for life, am I sure of that, how can I be sure of that.

"I've messed up every relationship I've ever been in," he says. "I don't want to mess this up."

"How could you possibly mess this up?" I ask.

"You don't know me. You'll see—I'll mess this up," he says.

"Well, don't this time, then."

"OK, but I always do. I always mess things up. Don't let me, don't let me hurt you."

"Hurt me?" I ask. "What are you gonna do to me?"

"I can tell you Lizzie, seriously, whatever happens I never meant to hurt you. I love you, I'm just a fuck-up."

"Nick, you're being ridiculous," I say. "What exactly are you afraid of doing to me?"

"I don't know, sweetie; you don't know me. You are the sweetest, most wonderful woman I know. . . . I have some things I'm still working out."

"That's OK. Everybody does. I do, too."

"You don't understand," he says. "You're so young."

"Don't say that. That's stupid."

"Don't let me fuck this up, Lizzie. Say it again. Say you love me but say I, Lizzie Simon, love you, Nicholas Berenson."

He's crazy, I think. But I say it.

"I, Lizzie Simon, love you, Nicholas Berenson."

DETOUR: My Bipolar Road Trip in 4-D

THE HORSIES IN OUR HEADS

Great Magnetism.

In their lives,
on this earth,
in general society
on highways
in parking lots
country clubs
forests, too,
Bipolar people must keep a reign on things,
mentally I mean
on the inside I mean.
There, there, horsies, I know ya each wanna go yer
own way, but c'mon just pick one way,
all together now!

Now.

Two bipolar people together,
loving each other,
understanding each other,
it's bound to set some things free,
BOOM SHAKA!!!
unlatch the barn doors
YEEEEEEE HAAAAAAA!!!!!
shake some shit up,
Did SOMEBODY SCREAM?!!?
disturb plate tectonics.
It's bound to come unbound
to turn the forest trees blue and gaseous
so that horsies on a rampage
can just gallop wildly
right on
like they were riding in the sky.

I'm in the car, on the road, heading from Providence, Rhode Island, to Washington, DC.

It's white, my dad's car: an SUV with maroon interiors. It feels big and spacious, peaceful and clean. I feel as if I could spend a long time in here.

I love driving. I love to drive. I only wish DC were farther away.

Could I be a trucker?

Maybe.

Could I cart cargo?

Why not.

I could drive for three days straight, and it's not even pretty outside.

There is no theater on my back. No productions to manage.

No one will recognize me this whole trip.

It's just me, my mix tapes, my cell phone, and the road.

Heaven isn't too far away.

What a relief.

I have no itinerary, no formal methodology, no structured sense of criteria, no strategy for interrogation.

This feels like freedom.

I want to figure this out as I go.

I will stay in motels, or occasionally with friends. I will write as I go, and use my free time to transcribe the interviews into my computer.

I will arrive in a town, call around to the mental health associations in the area, inquire about support group meetings, visit these meetings, and find and meet a young person there to interview. I want to hear stories about diagnosis, recovery, survival, and stigma.

I may not know exactly who I am looking for, but I will know it when I meet them. I will just know.

I have planned my first interview through a friend's friend. A performer I worked with at the Flea knew someone who has a sister in DC who is bipolar and successful. Her name is Marissa, she's twenty-nine, and she will be my first road trip subject.

I'm nervous, I suppose. I want to get this right.

I ring Marissa's doorbell.

She opens the door.

She's so pretty, with lovely light green eyes. Her hair is pulled back off her face. She's black, which I didn't know from our phone conversation.

"Welcome, Lizzie," she says cheerily as she guides me inside.

She's little, maybe five feet tall, and dressed casually. Her energy is open and calm.

I know from the second I meet her: this is going to be fine.

She sets us up in her kitchen. She's cut mangoes and made green tea. Her apartment is spacious and still; from the kitchen I can see through to the living room and into the bedroom. There are nice things everywhere: nice furniture, nice candles, nice framed photographs. The place is clean and orderly. The light is nice in here, too: warm and soft.

I pull my recorder out and ask her to introduce herself and tell me a little bit about her background.

She tells me she's adopted. Her biological father is African American; her biological mother, European Spanish. She was adopted by a single woman named Danielle from a "hard-to-place" agency along with her Chinese sister, Lisa. When Marissa was two, Danielle died in a car accident, and Marissa and Lisa went to live with Danielle's brother and his family of four. She and her sister were raised as part of his family.

Marissa was diagnosed with bipolar disorder after a manic episode she had when she was a freshman at a small women's college in California, during orientation.

"I had all of these big plans to go to California," she says. "I was sure things would be different from high school, and then— how do I say this? Shit flew in my face."

In high school, Marissa says she was very unhappy. Her parents suggested that she go to a therapist, and she went. But she didn't like it, and she stopped going.

"If they had insisted, this whole thing could have been avoided," she says.

"Really?" I ask.

"Well, probably not," she says.

We both wonder if there could ever be a sure diagnosis of bipolar disorder in the absence of a traumatic episode, because you can make excuses for the milder symptoms. *She's just being dramatic. She's just moody. She's just heartbroken. She's just an outsider.*

"I think for me, there were certain triggers that set it off, and I think one of them was the experience of seeing my father decline rapidly because of a stroke."

"You think your episodes were triggered by your dad's being sick?" I ask, incredulously.

"I think so."

"And if you had stayed in therapy you would have dealt with it and not been bipolar?"

She doesn't know, she says.

"In high school I was grappling with seeing all of the effects on him, and that was very hard, very upsetting, so it had me up and down a lot—always afraid that something worse was going to happen, that he was going to get sick again or that he was going to die.

"But it wasn't until I left DC and went all of the way to California and really had a lot of pangs of homesickness and was feeling . . . detached and disconnected . . ." Marissa struggles with finding the beginning of her story. "All the while I was enjoying being in this new place. . . . I think it opened up a lot of room for discovery, but also for confusion. And things got all sort of collapsed."

In her third week of college, Marissa says the mania started. "I just got into a really stressed-out, sped-up mode." She was sleeping less and less, aware that something was not right but not sure what that was.

"Insecurities started coming out," Marissa tells me. She spewed homophobic comments, paranoid, believing that all the girls were lesbians. Marissa's voice is now wavering and edgy.

I don't push her for the gory details.

Marissa remembers being filled with anger at the world. She says she was throwing her belongings in her dorm room and doing a lot of shadow boxing. Eventually, officials at the college evacuated her residence hall so that the paramedics could enter, grab her, strap her down, bring her to a hospital, and tranquilize her. There she waited zombie-like for her older brother to come fetch her. He spent a day packing her dorm room and then brought her home, back East.

"Well, not home," she says nervously, wiping her hands on her pants.

He drove her directly to a hospital, where her mother, her sister-in-law, and her godmother were waiting to break it to her that she would have to stay there for a while.

"We are admitting you," her mom said, and Marissa lost it and began to sob.

"I remember thinking, I have already been through hell, and now I am being dropped off at the loony bin."

I ask her if she thought then that things would ever be OK again.

"Yeah, I think I did," she says. "I was pretty determined to go back to school. That was a way for me to normalize the situation. I didn't want to quit. I didn't want to go to another school. I specifically wanted to go back to where I started. So yeah, I think I did have a sense that somehow things were going to be OK again."

I'm stunned that she went back. "How?"

"I think I just kind of decided that I had to get back there to get my life back."

Marissa says she is highly capable of confronting things, that she has survival skills that kick in, that being a stubborn person, a proud person, made her want to recover.

"I also had certain things going for me," she adds. "Some of those things have to do with basic privileges: wealth, education, a strong family support system, psychiatric resources. I come from a family where we happen to have a lot of family friends who are psychologists and psychiatrists and social workers, who were more equipped than an average group of people to deal with this type of thing. Because, you know, if we didn't have that kind of network we probably would have been scrambling a lot longer, and it would have been a bigger ordeal."

I ask Marissa what advice she would give to young people and their families.

"I would advise someone who has just been told that they are manic depressive to learn as much as possible. The more you know, the more aware you're going to be of your condition. Learn a lot about medication, and figure out what's comfortable for you: are you comfortable being in therapy, or are you comfortable seeing somebody just for medication, and then doing your own kind of personal therapy? It's really self-knowledge: teach yourself, understand yourself, understand this condition for what it is, always be searching to discover more, either on your own or from people. Kinda like what you're doing, Lizzie. Don't be afraid to ask other people; well, how do you experience this, what has your situation been like?"

"I think parents need to do the same thing," she says, continuing. "They need to learn as much as possible. It's important for parents to be given the tools to read what bipolar symptoms are so that they can be on the lookout. That way they're not just on this perpetual mode of OK: crisis, and then we come in."

I ask Marissa how she would convince someone bipolar to take medicine.

"That's a good question. I don't know. For me, once I realized how grave the situation was . . . I never liked the idea of being sick. But I don't know how you would make somebody. People just have to realize they are gonna hit a wall, and if they don't realize that, then they are just going to keep hitting a wall. Do you let somebody keep hitting a wall? I guess you have to."

We wrap up, and Marissa tells me she's looking for a new job. She was grant writing for a nearby public high school, trying to fund programs that the DC public school system doesn't support, like day care centers for teen mothers and teen pregnancy prevention programs. She's looking to do something still involving urban minority communities, but she wants to be less hands-on. She thinks she'd might like to work in the community affairs department of a corporation.

"I know how to take care of myself now. That's been the biggest thing. Bigger than getting medicated. I know how to avoid triggers, how to keep myself safe."

"What kind of triggers?"

"Anything. Manipulative people, or overwhelming responsibilities, or . . . you know, dating the wrong kind of guys."

I smile. "I never do that!" I say, and she smiles shyly back.

We talk about how we still experience being bipolar even though we're on medicine. How manias and depressions "leak" through our meds and continue to remind us of our mercurial nature. How we're trying to listen for biochemical and psychological internal cues, but how it's hard to tell the difference sometimes.

I say I feel as if I'm surfing, moving myself in all sorts of subtle ways just to stay on the board and enjoy the waves. It's the very first time I've articulated that to anyone out loud, and it creates an intense neediness within me. I sort of want her to understand everything, absolutely everything, every feeling, every thought, every experience, every relationship I've ever had. . . . She quickly says she feels like that too. She says it calmly, and it relieves me.

I could not have anticipated that talking to other bipolar people might shake me up in ways I am not ready to handle. Even with this peaceful meeting. Even with the optimism it has brought me.

I can feel something weird happening. Already.

Nick calls me at least a dozen times a day.

I spend a few days in DC working on my interview with Marissa and making phone calls to mental health groups in different parts of the country. It exhausts me, this work: explaining my project over and over again; transcribing Marissa's interview, her vulnerability, her strength. I feel like I just want to drive again.

After about an hour in the car, my mind starts to go around and around a very tiny carousel. I begin thinking about how Marissa returned to school after her manic episode, even though it was public and violent and humiliating. How important she said re-establishing herself was for her sense of self.

Going back was never an option for me. I begged to go to Paris again. My friends were there. But I was under watch my senior spring of high school. It felt like a holding cell. I understand why my parents wanted to protect me. But it really sucked. My mom was always on my case about my weight and my acne (both, side effects of the lithium); my dad made little contact with me, apart from medical journal articles he would slip under my bedroom door. I resented them both.

Maybe we all should have had therapy, I think.

Because after that period, I didn't ever return home for more than a couple of days.

I start to remember things, driving along. Thanksgiving meals when I'm in near tears the whole time. Fresh from college with a million stories to share but suddenly silent, mopey, on edge. Everybody, it seems, is dancing around the house—my parents, our many guests, my brothers, their friends. They are in color; I am in black and white. I am in slo-mo. Something is growing inside me, taking up more and more space within me, like a balloon expanding, pushing my organs around. I am ruining Thanksgiving with my incapacity to Just Be Normal when DAMN IT, I had just been normal up there at school. Why couldn't everyone see me there? I'm horrible here.

Wait . . . just drive. . . .

Just to be on the safe side, keep them the hell away from us, OK?

97

I figured out how to not be there for very long. I didn't communicate my strategy to my parents, which made them act testy whenever I asked for a ride to the bus station.

I've got an exam, I'd say. Or a radio show.

But they knew. My father recoiled further. My mother lashed out. Screaming matches made sore losers out of us both.

I didn't have it in me to deal with absolutely everything and remake my head into a stable home. My strategy was to make my surroundings safe for my homeless head. And to exit whenever I felt unsafe.

Wait. . . .

But we were all more or less homeless in college. We slept in our rooms but studied in libraries, ate in common rooms or restaurants, and had most of our life experience outside our dorms. That was OK for me because I didn't know how to build a home.

Wait.

My room was always a mess. Food containers on table tops, dirty laundry and trash covering the floor. Days passed without showers. But being a grungy college student was nothing abnormal.

When I started producing with my punky head of butchered hair, I moved into a two-bedroom apartment with my cousin, Julia, an artist. She set up immediately; she hung her paintings, arranged photos of friends and family all over the house, unpacked her kitchen appliances. Within twenty-four hours, Julia's bedroom walls were covered in multicolored postcards, fabric samples, sketches. Her things. She made it into her home.

I didn't know how to do that. I had thrown my kitchenware down the dorm garbage chute in a childish refusal to pack and leave college. The walls of my room in that apartment remained bare and white until I moved out a year later, and most of my belongings were still in boxes. I used the place to sleep, not to live. I lived at the theater, ate my meals there or in restaurants. Went to see shows at night all over the city. I remember dishes not done for weeks, bills unpaid because I never opened my mail. More days without taking showers. Months without doing laundry. I remember disturbing Julia.

Stop. . . .

I craved stability but remained homeless and unkempt. My mind could never focus on the little things: cleaning up, filing my own papers, building my nest. I was otherly devoted.

I could give of myself completely to work. But why was it, why is it so weird and hard to shower and clean up my shit every day, to hang out with kids my age who do things that kids my age are supposed to do, to take care of myself and my life in the most normal basic human way?

Marissa goes back when she makes a mess, and she cleans it up! Marissa is devoted to herself! Marissa doesn't care about getting in the papers!

Any effort I make to build a regular, paced, balanced, adult life—even with something as microcosmic as cleaning my house or hanging out with my family—brings on a freakish panic!

I'm just a little rat on a wheel—no, no, I'm a little rat who knows how to produce in a messy cage fooling everybody! But for how long!

Stop!

Suddenly the car is too small.

Suddenly there are no good songs on any station.

Suddenly the road seems endless and bleak.

I have so much farther to go, I think, and the idea chokes me, sucks up my fresh air.

We know what they look like. We know what they're up to, and we know that it's no good.

FUCK!! OFF!!

Wait.

Stop.

I check into a motel room and call Davide, an old friend from high school who lives in Parkertown, Virginia. He says I can come and stay with him for as long as I like. I decide I will, and I get under the covers to take a nap. It is dinnertime, but I figure I will go and grab some McDonalds after I rest.

Except that I wake up the next morning.

On my way to Parkertown, I remember being upset the night before, being really hard on myself. About what? I think. Marissa doesn't need to be a model for me. She plays it safe. She has no ambition. She sees triggers everywhere. She's been fully therapized.

As I drive I try to mock trigger theorists everywhere.

There is nothing I need to avoid.

The world is my oyster, not the darkness under my bed.

I am not afraid of anything, and you don't need to be either.

My left hand is on the wheel; my right is nervously twirling my hair so hard that strands are falling out, locking twisted into my fingers or drifting slowly to the floor of the car.

Nick calls. He starts to nag me about what I am doing after I finish this project. He offers me the opportunity to convert his land in Schroon Lake into an arts colony. I am ambivalent, but I call him back with a strategy four minutes later: Research other colonies and seek partnerships, with foundations or something.

Nicholas has the idea that we should seek partnership with New York University. His parents are on the board.

"My mom flipped for the idea, Lizzie; she's ready to go!" He's very excited: "You could have your own arts colony, Lizzie. You would be so happy!"

It would be so exciting to work with Nick, I think. His energy is as great as mine. We could really make things happen.

But I have a change of heart. Suddenly, instinctively.

"I can't really do it, Nick. I don't want to work for you," I say. "Or your family."

He's annoyed. He doesn't let it go.

Nick does the dangle. "I'm getting Rick to be one of your brother's clients," he says.

Bunny look at this carrot, he says; don't move your eyes from the carrot.

Baby, I want to say, put that carrot away. It's you I want. I mean it. I know it. I want you. I need you. I'm so tired of being lonely, Nick; you are the only one who knows who I am. Put the fucking carrot down, get over here, let's take our shirts off and lie down. I want to hear your heart and touch your shoulder. Just stop talking. Put your arms around me; let's just lie here and breathe.

I'm in a library in Parkertown, Virginia, killing time, reading.

I figure that even if I don't find a bipolar person in Parkertown, I can still hang out with Davide. We haven't seen each other in years.

Davide doesn't know I'm bipolar. I managed to graduate without letting my secret out. So I don't know how exactly to talk to him about my book. I could pretend I just find bipolar people fascinating or something. Maybe.

But I'm finally at the "far, far away" I imagined back in Brooklyn. I have unlimited time, space, and freedom to think about things. Except that it doesn't quite feel like I thought it would.

Just then, my cell phone rings. I answer it, and a few ladies in the library glare at me.

It's a woman from one of the mental health organizations I called.

She says she has someone for me to interview in Parkertown!

Someone she says is really cool, positive and young!

She's setting it up for tomorrow!

Oh my God! I think. This is going to work!

Davide takes me out to dinner, and we catch up.

When we were in high school he was technically my brother's friend; he graduated two years before me. Davide was one of the more unusual, intelligent guys at Providence Academy. I remember hearing his laughter breaking the stifling Providence Academy stasis from all sides of campus. People thought he was a nut, but they liked having him around. I was unhappily dating or pining after Chace through most of high school, but I was always much closer to Davide. When Chace decided in my sophomore year to take the boarding school girl to the prom, I was devastated. I went with Davide instead. He still carries our prom picture in his wallet.

Davide keeps saying how psyched he is that I am in Parkertown. He's heard all sorts of versions of rumors about what I'm up to.

"This is so Lizzie Simon," he says. He tells me how he had told all of his friends in Parkertown about me. He says he had a ton of people he wanted me to meet, that they all knew about little Lizzie Simon.

It feels so good to be treated like a cherished sparkling magic trick of a girl. It's my favorite thing.

Davide starts asking about my research, and I awkwardly explain it to him without revealing anything personal, although he's certainly smart enough to figure it out, and my half-telling of the facts only creates a weird third yucky person at the dinner table. I could just out and tell him, but that's what the night would turn into: my sordid tales and his not knowing how to react or what to say. And that's not the night I want.

I don't really want him to know. He thinks of me as a great kid, and it means a lot to me.

I ask him if he knows anybody who is bipolar.

"Do they have to be clinically diagnosed," he asks, "or can I just have a hunch?"

"Clinically diagnosed," I say, and giggle.

"Oh that's too bad," he says. "Sounds a lot like me."

It's true. I don't know Davide enough to know about his lows, but his highs are legendary among the members of my family. He used to break into my house after midnight and demand that I go with him for a drive. I'd get out of bed and throw on some clothes. I think the only place that was open that late in Providence was Wings to Go, so we'd go there and just hang out. In most of my photographs of Davide, he's got a frying pan on his head or something.

He tells me he is dating someone but that it's not going so well. "She's very nice; she's great to talk to, but like, I'll do something and she'll be like, Davide! She just does not embrace the madness!"

I love Davide's energy. It might exhaust other people, but it's always been something I was very comfortable around. Davide makes me happy.

After dinner he drives me all over Parkertown and tells me about the stories he's working on as a journalist for the local paper. We don't talk about bipolar illness, but we don't need to. He doesn't see it as part of me, and for tonight, neither do I.

We're at a Chili's restaurant, at Jan's suggestion. She's addicted to one of their appetizers and needs a fix.

I arrived first and waited for her on a bench just outside. People walked in. They looked at me, I looked at them, and when they were women I looked a bit harder. Maybe Jan? No. Maybe Jan? Nope.

Soon a red sports car drove up with music blasting. The woman behind the wheel was rocking out in her own little world. It was Jan. She got out of her car, saw me waiting, grinned a bit, and said my name—not like a timid "Lizzie?" This was an assured pronouncement, as if my name were one of her favorite words to say: "LIZZIE."

Jan is really outgoing. When we walk into the restaurant together, I actually feel the atmosphere intensifying. She's just got the electricity, the charge, that thing. It's a power thing, an adventurer's inner constitution.

Jan blends into the landscape here in Parkertown. She has pale skin, pretty eyes, and wavy shoulder-length hair. She is dressed casually in brightly colored, baggy clothes.

Jan is in her early thirties, but she was diagnosed only four years ago. I ask her why it took so long.

"My career masks it," she says." My career allows me to be bouncing off the walls."

"Tell me about what you do," I say.

"I'm a radio announcer. I do a morning show, and I've been doing it for years. It's funny; my dad says he can't believe I get paid for doing this, for acting stupid and playing music all day. He says you used to do that when you were a kid, and nobody paid ya! But it's a whole lotta fun. Rock and roll, you know, craziness. . . ."

"So have you been manic on the radio before?"

"Oh gosh yes. Yeah. The thing about it is, me and my partner on the show, we're just back and forth," she snaps her fingers five times quickly, "and my brain is like a pinball going ninety miles an hour."

"So how is it that you can have a public radio show and be out of your mind, and nobody's taking you to the hospital?"

"Because it was just fun. It just looked fun and spontaneous and free. Of course, you know the whole rest of the world didn't realize that I was getting speeding tickets every time I got in the car, didn't realize that I had six hundred dollars in overdraft charges, in *overdraft* charges—that's not counting the amount that the check was for."

"What kinds of things did you do when you were manic?"

She leans in and speaks more softly. "One time, I was with a friend and we took a police car. . . . She was on drugs; I was just manic. We were in this little town, and the cop had a thing for some woman in McDonalds, so he was in McDonalds talking to this woman. . . . And what is this? Leaving your keys in your car? So we took his car for a spin, brought it back. He never knew. I should be dead or incarcerated right now, most definitely."

"Were those your glory days?" I ask her. I really hope she's not gonna feed me that *I love my manias* line. It's all bullshit. People trying to elevate bullshit, to give meaning to bullshit.

She raises one eyebrow. "After the three weeks of mania is over, you've got all of these little fires to put out. It looks like you're just having a great time, and you're feeling like you're having a great time. But once it's over, it's like what have I done, and who have I done it with? There's a lot of promiscuity that comes along with it. Things that I would never do if I weren't manic."

Like what? I was thinking, but I couldn't ask. Dirty stuff. Jan was probably naughty with men she shouldn't have been naughty with. I just nod, and she continues.

"No, I don't want to run off and buy three hundred dollars worth of duct tape, which I did at one point. I bought two hundred dollars worth of purple embroidery thread, too. And I didn't cross-stitch anything!"

"What? It must have been boxes and boxes of it!"

"The really amazing thing is that I don't ever cross-stitch!"

"Why did you buy it?" I ask.

"I walked through the store and went, Oh my god that's pretty! Tada! And I just happened to have two hundred some odd dollars in my pocket. Shades of purple, that's all I got."

"Is there any reason why purple?" I ask.

"Look, just because it's there, and there's no place between point A and point B where there's a thought process. Finally I said I don't want to do this anymore. I want to be able to make choices based on what's best."

"Tell me about your diagnosis," I say.

"OK. I had gotten into recovery for an eating disorder and a drug addiction."

I nod. "What drug?"

"Speed. It leveled me."

"So you identified yourself as having an eating disorder and a drug problem; you went to get help for that. . . ."

"Look, I passed out in the middle of the road, Lizzie. I was crossing the street and passed out in the middle of the road, got hit by a car, and came to with some Mexican dude cussin' me out. You haven't lived till you've woken up to some Mexican dude cussin' you out."

"Why'd you pass out?"

"Not enough food."

"You got hit by a car."

"I got hit by a car, and I said this isn't working for me any more." Jan starts laughing. "Maybe it's time to do something. Let's just see what life is like without throwing up. So I went and got help for that, went into rehab. It was kind of a lot to do at one time, and it was Thanksgiving and Christmas, no less, where you get to go and be with family, and of course all you want to do is be high and throw up and escape. So I got into therapy. And my doctor happened to notice that I couldn't sit still there and I was walking on her sofa. High places—I'm into high places. When I'm manicky I love high places. I just like to be higher. I used to go up on the roof."

"I do that too when I'm manicky: climb things, scaffoldings, trees, sets, whatever's around. Did you think you could fly?" I ask her.

"I never thought I could fly, but I never thought I could fall. So anyway, I'm standing on my therapist's sofa, and she says 'I think you're bipolar.' And I say, 'Like hell I am!'" She laughs, and continues, "Kinda hard to convince somebody you're not manic when you're standing on their sofa."

Jan tells me she grew up in an abusive household, where she was forced to perform oral sex on her uncle in the shower when she was a little girl. I feel dizzy when she tells me this, but I try to just look her in the eye and stay steady. She doesn't have much contact with her family anymore, but she has her own small family: a son and a daughter, ages nine and eleven. Their father is not in the picture, and Jan doesn't seem to want to talk about him.

"So everybody at work must know you are bipolar," I say. "They've seen you manic; they must have known when you were going through recovery. No stigma at work?"

"No. I'm blessed to be in a situation where I can be very open about it. What I've found is that it's good in every area of my life to have someone who knows the situation. Like my boss knows, and my partner on the air knows."

"It doesn't feel strange for people to know?" I ask.

"No. But if you've not been given permission to walk in every day and ask me if I am taking my medication, then don't do it. Because it's going to tick me off. And I'm gonna say 'Bite me' and I'm not going to take it. There are a lot of issues in my life, and control is one of them. I've always said that I'm really lucky to be in a career that not only lets me be who I am but requires me to be who I am. It uses those wild traits. If I had to sit behind a desk I wouldn't be able to do it. I'd be unemployed. I'd be a wreck."

"What were you like as a kid? Did you feel different from other kids?"

"Definitely. I always felt like somebody forgot to give me the rule book. I was born, everybody else was handed a manual, and nobody handed one to me. And so I'm walking around making up my own rules as I go along here."

I tell Jan how I'm trying to collect testimonies and advice, and I ask her what she would offer if she could have direct influence on the lives of young bipolar people and their families.

"In general I would say, whatever decisions they can make on their own, let them make because there's so much of their lives that they're going to lose control of. So if they can decide something, let them do it. Choose your battles, basically."

"What else?"

"Get educated, really get educated. You can't do enough reading. I would also tell parents to take care of themselves and to make sure the other siblings are getting whatever attention they need. Someone with a mental illness is a high-maintenance person, and they can just sap you dry. Express how you feel. If you feel the person is being abusive, say, "Hey, you're being abusive," because chances are they're not trying to be abusive. Say it; just tell them."

"What kind of treatment works?"

"Well, I don't know. I can tell you I think hospitals are traumatic for people most of the time, and ineffective too. And I think that a lot of people feel safe there and don't get better because they can stay there. There are people where it's a revolving door. The things that I saw in the hospital . . . they're not proactive in their treatment, not at all. It's just a place for people to hang out. Sit there with your disorder, eat your meal, take your meds, go to sleep, a little art therapy—which is not art therapy at all, it's just here draw a picture—now go shoot hoops and play Ping-Pong. And as we all know, medical insurance for mental health sucks. Mine pays fifty percent up to five hundred dollars in a calendar year. Now, if you're going to a therapist, that's five weeks, and that's if you go once a week—that doesn't count med checks, doesn't count labs—it's ridiculous. And let me tell you something," she continues. "I am a strong believer that simply coping is for cowards. You need to go *get* what you want. You need to go *find* what's missing."

"What would you tell a person who was bipolar who was refusing to get treatment because they were like, I love who I am?"

"What I would say to them is that from my experience, treatment allows you to be who it is you are and who it is you want to be without the repercussions, without all the fires you have to put out. If you decide you want to drive a hundred twenty miles per hour, go ahead! You're still gonna go that fast, and you're still gonna get a ticket. But you decided it! You made the decision on your own instead of being controlled by something else. And you are being controlled by a chemical imbalance. You have a chemical thing that's keeping you from being everything you were meant to be. And I say that being someone who periodically says, I'm bored. I wanna go to the moon now."

"So what are you on now," I ask her. Marissa was taking a drug I had never even heard of. Her doctor was on the cutting edge of new medicines. Lots of bipolar people take a cocktail of different kinds of drugs, including antidepressants. Me, I find comfort taking the ancient generic lithium, and taking that alone.

"I take Depakote and Wellbutrin," Jan tells me.

"How do you feel?"

"Fine. Great, most of the time. I mean, the Depakote's caused me to gain weight, most definitely, which is really difficult for me, having an eating disorder. And sometimes I just get tired of the whole thing. Tired of having the label, tired of . . . Most of the time being different I love, but there are times when I think, you know, I just don't want to be this anymore. I don't want to go for the blood tests. I don't want to go for med checks. I don't want to take these stupid pills every day. Can we just play like I'm not bipolar for a little while? Sometimes it just gets frustrating."

"When you were diagnosed, were you worried that you

weren't going to have the kind of spontaneity that you had before?"

"Oh yeah. That was the frightening thing about becoming medicated. I didn't know what I was going to be left with, and am I going to be able to make a living off of it? What is really me? If you're telling me that all that I have done and been has been some kind of disorder, and you're going to cure me of my personality? It hasn't been just a matter of: I'm not going to have any fun. It's: I don't know what's me then, if this isn't it. It feels like everything's a lie."

"How would you account for your success?" I ask.

"I'm just really optimistic, and I'm really in awe of people's individuality, mine and everyone else's, and so I think that when I find I'm different, it doesn't necessarily make me feel bad that I'm not like everybody else. There are things I really like about myself. I like the fact that I can walk out into the sunshine and say: the air is great, the sun is great. It probably sounds very trite, but being alive is just a really cool thing. It's important to me not to miss anything. Just don't medicate me out of my personality, and I'll be fine."

Nicholas wakes me up in the middle of the night. I'm on Davide's foldaway bed, my cell phone on the pillow next to mine. I keep the cell phone close at all times except during the interviews, when I turn the thing off. I speak quietly, as to not wake Davide asleep in the next room.

Nick quickly becomes upset talking about the possibility of not knowing me forever, and he seems irrational, as if he isn't really listening to me. He is just skimming, and then he dives and descends and descends into this excruciating depression. He is sobbing and suicidal and says he has to get out of there. I don't really know what to do. I tell him to go to an all-night diner, or to call Albert or Jenny. Actually, I say "Call a friend," and he weeps, "I don't have any friends," and I say "Check yourself into a hospital." He just wants to die. I try to tell him, "You have a life, you have a job, a business," and he can't hear any of it.

"You have me!" I say. "I love you!"

He starts to say he is going to go to Parkertown, he is planning to visit me the next day, he is going to get rid of his apartment, he is tired of living in a box, in a city full of boxes. But he is just gone, and sobbing. He is serious; this is serious. I am imprisoned on the phone. I tell him he can't kill himself because I love him so much I can't continue to live without him, that I would never recover.

I have been on the other side. I was depressed like this when I was little, and thinking, if only they could see how much better it would be without me. I am just not fit for life.

He says he doesn't know what is happening.

I say that I do, that it is chemical, that it isn't his fault, that he needs help.

The whole thing probably lasts ten or fifteen minutes, and then all of a sudden he is OK, and saying this too shall pass, and apologizing over and over again.

When I finally fall asleep, I have nightmare after nightmare until morning comes.

I'm in a truck stop somewhere in Virginia, eating yummy eggs and hash browns and drinking really bad coffee.

I left Parkertown early this morning. I definitely could have stayed longer and hung out with Davide, but I have a support group meeting to go to tonight in Atlanta, and I can't skip it. Who knows if I'll get lucky, the way I did with Jan, in every town. I can't believe how little I planned this whole thing. Whatever balls I had in New York I don't have anymore. I have been neutered. I mean, it's not like producing shows. People simply don't return my phone calls here. I just assumed they would because they did in New York.

This is a different thing. It's really different.

I don't even have a single interview set up anywhere else in the country. I don't even know where I'm going after Atlanta. I really assumed that I was just going to hit the karmic lottery over and over again all over the United States of America. I'm beginning to wish I had a real itinerary. I mean, everybody keeps telling me that no one under thirty even goes to the support groups.

Breathe.

I'm really impressed with how open Jan says she is at work about her illness. I never wanted my boss, Jim, to know. When I gave notice, he didn't ask me what my project was about, so I didn't offer the information. I just said I wanted to travel and write.

One day a few weeks before I left the Flea, he came into work and asked me what this bipolar thing was all about. He had just come from his therapist's office and asked about it there. I guess he had overheard me mentioning the project over the phone, and maybe he was talking in therapy about my leaving the Flea. It felt weird for him to suddenly take an interest.

I didn't want to discuss it with him. He had been so sweet during my last weeks of work. He wrote a glowing letter in the program about me, and he kept telling people he could never replace me. We were having a good time together. The show we were doing was a hit.

But he wanted to talk about it with me.

"I had no idea," he kept saying. He looked at as if I were a mystery. Like, here is this young girl whom I've spent more time with this year than my own family, and I don't know this very major part of her life.

It pained me to think of him racking his brains to remember clues that would point to this. It pained me to have this man I had killed myself to impress know something very dark about me.

I had been the calm in every storm, but I felt my image tainted as we stood there, awkwardly, together.

"I'm very healthy now," I said. "There'd be no way for you to know, Jim."

He just looked at me. "My psychiatrist told me you must have a really mild case," he said.

"Yeah," I said. I just nodded and got back to work.

Stop.

In Atlanta I visit a support group meeting, hoping to find a young person to interview.

I'm on the inside of a huge medical complex, in the parking lot of a geriatric care facility. This is where the meeting is supposed to be. The complex is on a long stretch of road filled with hospitals. Children's hospitals, specialty care clinics, the Centers for Disease Control.

The drive here makes my skin itch. I hate hospitals.

And I'm fifteen minutes early.

I have been driving for nine hours straight. I had no idea that Atlanta was so far away from Parkertown. I drove all day, and I almost didn't make it in time for the meeting.

It's not bad, driving. I listen to a lot of music, and my thoughts relax, and it's pretty peaceful.

But now that I'm at the complex, I'm tweaked. My legs are shaking, and I feel jittery in the head.

I'm really nervous. I don't really know why, except maybe because I hate hospitals and maybe because I hate support groups. I remember I found one that met at a hospital in New York when I was at Columbia. And I asked my mom to come to town so we could go together. And we went. And everybody was old—her age. And they had lost jobs, and husbands, and girlfriends. And I watched my mom grow more and more concerned as the meeting went on.

"You don't really have anything to do with those people," she said to me afterward.

I wasn't so sure. But the kind of support I needed wasn't available there; that we agreed on.

Time passes. I do handstands in the parking lot. I read once that ants probably experience less stress because the blood in their bodies doesn't have to fight gravity to reach the brain. It makes me think of all of the acrobatic dancers I know, and it occurs to me that, generally speaking, the people I know who spend a considerable amount of time upside down are pretty mellow and happy. And it works, handstands. You feel better after.

But I'm still really anxious.

Eventually around twenty people show up. We're meeting in a small bland conference room. I take a seat.

The meeting starts, and a guy introduces himself as the leader. He fumbles his papers and nervously strokes his balding head. He begins reporting facts and stats into the air as the group stares bewildered in his direction.

What have I got myself into?

He probably has the right intentions. I mean, he volunteers to do these groups, and that's awfully nice of him, but he couldn't ever persuade me to do anything. If I were in need, if I were confused, if I needed guidance, I wouldn't put my confidence in him. Plus he is unipolar. Unipolars just get depression. It's a mixed meeting of unipolars and bipolars.

Anyway, he is in his fifties and he is the group leader, but there's also this woman, Mary, who is clearly very involved. She doesn't seem to think he should be the leader either. She doesn't say so explicitly, but she's sort of rolling her eyes at him, undermining him. Mary's young and bright and pretty, and she's got lots of energy. She's bipolar.

We are supposed to go around the room and each talk for about a minute. Mary starts.

She is all excited because she has just come back from a conference on St. Simons Island and heard an expert talk about how many mental illnesses, in fact, are not biological. This expert says that they are just spiritual crises, that the current wave of diagnosis and drug treatment is a big conspiracy among doctors and pharmaceutical companies.

"Maybe I don't have to be on medicine for the rest of my life!" she says, her eyes so juiced they start to tear.

Well, the leader does not like this one bit. He says this expert goes against the belief of the meetings, which is that mental illnesses are biological disorders treated with medicine. But it is too late. Lots of people in the meeting are really into Mary's idea: that they are just experiencing a spiritual crisis, that they might be

able to be healed spiritually, not biochemically. More than anything in the world, people coming to terms with mental illness
like hearing exactly what Mary's telling them: that they're not
really mentally ill.

"They've done studies," Mary says dismissively to the leader.

"Well," he retorts, "I'd surely like to see those studies."

The next woman talks about another "cure" for bipolar illness
she has heard about.

"A clinic in Georgia," she says, "where they actually retrain
your brain not to be bipolar. It's called biofeedback or something.
It's like a video game; you just have to concentrate on it while
your brain is hooked up to a monitor. Usually it's people at their
wit's end who go there. It's their final hope."

The only person questioning this stuff is the leader librarian
guy, and he's too annoying to ally with. I stay quiet.

I am thinking about the kid who has just been diagnosed,
this imaginary kid, the kid I'm doing all this research for, this
kid I have in my head who is going to rock the world if she can
get good treatment and recover. I'm thinking about how difficult
it is to get sound information and coherent advice. I'm thinking,
gee, if she tries to reach out and get some information, and if she
calls a mental health organization in her area, she'll end up somewhere like here.

As people speak I consider them for my project. Most of them
are too old, or too, well, weird.

A young guy talks next about his depressive episodes. He
works with refugees getting them jobs. He's young and bipolar,
but he's been on and off meds for years; and he says he is off them
at the meeting. Veto: I need people committed to treatment.

The next woman is in her fifties, and she's depressed. Her
husband is there. She starts to cry. She's about to lose her job, and
this keeps happening, and what is wrong with her, she just wants
to know.

Then a handsome, fancy German woman starts talking about
her bipolar schizoaffective son. She has no clinical diagnosis her-

self, but I identify her immediately as a real nut. She is here to get information and "to see what other people with this problem look like." Her son isn't getting any better, no matter what they put him on. "He just sits in his room and does nothing," she says with a tone of disgust.

Maybe he just hates you, I think.

A woman who hasn't spoken yet introduces herself as the mother of Matt, a young guy sitting beside her. Matt looks like a football player out of central casting. He's a big guy. A big, normal as normal gets, looking guy.

His mom addresses the German lady, telling her they tried different drugs on Matt for almost three years before he found the right thing and became better. She says she stood by him every day. She went to every doctor's appointment. She came home from work on her lunch hours to keep him company; she just would not give up for almost three years.

"I can't wait that long," the German lady says. She's come with her boyfriend, a handsome guy, also wealthy looking.

Next is this crackpot bipolar nutritionist lady who says that at the Parsons Institute they taught her how to change her diet and do eight million behavioral adjustments so she doesn't need so much medicine. She is fifty-nine, not young enough for my purposes.

Next is a lady whose bipolar husband is in a mental institution that she really likes. He has tried to commit suicide a few times, she says, and this hospital is giving him the treatment he needs. She wants to share this information with the group because so many people have horror stories about hospitals. I'm happy to see someone on the side of patiently loving and supporting the mentally ill.

Next is a stuttering young black woman. She tells a story about going into her HMO, telling them she's depressed, being handed a prescription for meds five minutes later, with no therapy and no consultation. She smiles. "It works," she says. "I guess I shouldn't complain."

Next is a disheveled church lady counting on God to bring her out of this. No one comments.

Then speaks a big African lady who just laughs through her talk. It is odd, but I like her. I mean after all, why not add a gorgeous giggling two-hundred-pound bipolar woman in afrocentric costume? She's complaining that she can't find a job, and the guy who works with refugees sitting next to me says he thinks he can help her with that. Her eyes light up, and she keeps giggling.

And then Matt and his mother talk. They are just smart, good people who make sense and have a success story to tell.

The meeting is over shortly thereafter. I go up to Matt and ask him if I can interview him, and he says sure, as long as it's confidential. We arrange to meet in Gainesville the next day for lunch.

I don't like these support group meetings. People in great need sit in a circle and share unscientific dangerous information. But if that's what it takes to meet someone, fine.

I drive an hour outside of Atlanta to meet Matt in his hometown of Gainesville. He's picked a really charming cafe, which sits inside an old house. It's about three o'clock, so the place is empty. We order coffee. When the waitress is safely out of earshot, Matt leans into my tape recorder and introduces himself.

"OK. My name's Matt, and I'm twenty-four, and I've lived in Gainesville for about seventeen years. I'm between colleges right now, working at an independent bookstore in town. I've been working there full time since August."

His voice wavers a bit. "I've been stable for about a year now. I'm taking an atypical antipsychotic called Clozaril and two antidepressants, Effexor and Paxil, and Xanax for anxiety attacks. For the most part, I'm doing all right now, better than I have been for the past four or five years."

"How does it feel in your head right now?"

"Peaceful, quiet. If I have to take these drugs for the rest of my life, that's fine with me. I feel relaxed," he says. "I like to think I'm thinking a lot more clearly. I have about three or four panic attacks a week, but I feel more rested than I have in years. Not in control, but less out of control. Two years ago at this time, I felt I was on a freight train. I couldn't steer it. I couldn't stop it. Now it's more like driving a car. You can see everything around you; you can see things coming before they get to you. It's a relief to be at this stage."

"What does it mean to you to be bipolar?"

"I think of it as a roller coaster ride," he says. "I have only had one manic episode, and that was when I was in college. I remember it was as if I could do no wrong. Everything I did was superhuman. I was beyond the laws of physics."

Matt looks me straight in the eye when he speaks to me. His voice is deep, and he speaks in fluid complete sentences.

"Mostly my problem has been with depression, and the word I would use to describe that best is hopelessness. It's like being inside a bottomless pit, and not being able to see the light at the top. I only have one nightmare when I have nightmares, and it's always the same. It's being alone, in the dark, screaming, and nobody can hear me. And that's what's it's like being that depressed. I couldn't communicate to anybody what I was feeling. I felt maybe if I could describe it, I could exorcise it. But it defied definition. I just went through the motions, taking all the medicine I was prescribed. I was beyond despair. Despair is a feeling that nothing will ever get better. I was so far gone that it was like nothing ever had been better."

The waitress comes and brings our coffee. I wait till she's gone to speak again.

"So how were you diagnosed? What happened?"

"I remember it was like a crash, spring of my sophomore year at college. I went immediately from high to low within twenty-four hours. I was taking a religion class. I was really interested in that sort of thing: Biblical archeology. I thought it would help if I knew Greek. So I sat down and tried to teach myself to read Greek. It's amazing how much I actually did learn. I felt energized all the time. I didn't need any sleep. I put off long involved projects and did them at the last minute because I felt I didn't need the extra time. I tried out for and got major parts in two school plays. Didn't do any of my homework because I was too thrilled with being on the stage."

"How long did this last?"

"About three months. I wrote a lot of letters to the editor of the local paper about bizarre things; for instance, a very long rambling story about the Vietnam War. In the middle of the term, I crashed, and I don't really know what caused it, but after twenty-four hours I was on the other side of the spectrum completely. I withdrew from all of my classes and went home, and that's when I started sleeping. All of the time. I didn't communicate with any friends. I was afraid. I was particularly afraid of communication by phone. I don't know why."

"I went to a theologically conservative college. A lot of my friends believed that anything could be solved by prayer. I almost believed it myself for a while, until I hit rock bottom. I fell by the wayside as far as the prayer groups, and I felt my friends had a tremendous sense of pity for me. And that bothered me. Especially that kind of pity, you know: 'he's fallen by the wayside.' It's not their fault, they're set in the ways that they were raised. But I was very lonely.

"Also, while I was manic, I managed to alienate a lot of my friends, so they weren't there for me when I hit bottom. I had been depressed in high school, but it was nothing like this. There was no escape. I never attempted suicide, though I thought about it a lot. I didn't want to die. I wanted to be happy, but I just couldn't see how that was possible any more.

"So I spent the next two or three years at home trying all sorts of medicine, and ECT, too."

"What was that like?" I ask him.

"Well, I had seen *One Flew Over the Cuckoo's Nest,* and I'd seen how they did that, and I was terrified. But sort of on a distant level. I was so depressed that everything seemed to be happening to somebody else, and not to me. A few times, it was very, very scary."

"What do they do?"

"What they do is they put you on a gurney. They strap you down. Then they give you a muscle relaxant so when the electricity hits you you don't have a seizure. They give you a fast-acting barbiturate to knock you out for five minutes. Then they run a low-amp current through your brain with electrodes on either side of your head. A psychiatrist takes care of the procedure, and there's an anesthesiologist present. They take all the necessary precautions to make it as comfortable as possible. It was still very, very frightening. It wasn't really the electricity that scared me; it was being knocked out and thinking that I might not wake up. I remember my parents insisted on being with me when I was in the recovery room. It was sort of against hospital policy, but they managed it. It made me very, very sick. It gave me a terrible headache. It took two or three hours to recover. I went through two series of ten treatments. The first one was in the fall two years ago, every other day for ten treatments in the morning."

"Did it do anything?" I ask him.

"It did, actually. The first series was successful. I felt a lot better after it was over. But then I started to relapse, so we had to do another series. And that seemed to work, but not as well as the first series. So then my doctor decided to put me on a maintenance dose, once every four or five weeks. It turned out that the benefit wasn't worth the side effects."

Right. He's so calm.

"Then I started on Clozaril, and I pretty much stuck with it until it took effect about a year later. And it really wasn't because I had any kind of particular faith in my doctor; I really didn't care."

"You'd given up," I said.

"Yeah. I don't even remember all of the names of the drugs I've taken. Tried lithium, Depakote, Tegretol, Noroton."

"What's a trial period like?" I ask him. "You go on something and wait?"

"Yeah, a few weeks."

"So you just sit around and wait and see if anything's gonna happen?"

"Yeah, it depended on which drug we were using. Some of them have different periods of time before they start taking effect."

"It must have been so frustrating," I say.

"It was. It was. And I'm glad I cannot remember exactly how I felt."

"Your mom said last night that you slept for a year."

"Yep, pretty much. I'd wake up in the morning around eleven, take a nap after lunch, go to bed early. My doctor had used this particular drug with lots of patients. He knew it was going to take a long time to take effect, and it was about a year before the side effects went away. Really weird side effects: I was wetting the bed every night; I was drooling on my pillow."

"You must have just felt like one of those crazy people in the hospital."

"Pretty much. In high school, I read a Don DeLillo play called *The Day Room,* and I felt like I was in the day room. And then about a year ago the medicine really started to take effect."

"You seem really well; you seem really clear-minded. What were you like as a kid?"

"As a kid . . . I had a tremendous amount of frustration in elementary school. I took things very, very personally."

"You were ultrasensitive?" I ask him.

"Yeah, I took myself extremely seriously. Any little thing that happened felt like somebody was doing this to me on purpose. Middle school was hell. I was teased a lot because I did well in school, and I took that very personally. It got to the point where this one particular kid was getting to me so much that I actually came home one day and asked my parents to help me kill him. I'd always had a tremendous amount of anxiety, a tremendous amount of frustration with other people and with myself, ever since I was very, very little. And I just thought everybody felt miserable all of the time. It took me years to realize that what I was feeling was not normal. My mom is always talking about how difficult life was for me when I was really young."

"But you feel pretty successful now?"

"Yeah, I guess I would say that."

I tell Matt that I'm looking to find out what went right in successful people rather than looking at what goes wrong in all of the destructive or suicidal cases of bipolar people. I tell him that I think young successful bipolar people have something unique to offer the universe, something special for other people like us. "How do you account for your success?"

"Well, my parents have stood by me ever since I was diagnosed. Unquestionably, unconditionally. Now, before there was a thought that I might have a chemical disorder, my parents were very frustrated with me. There were days when I absolutely could not go to school, and I would go to them in tears. They couldn't figure out what was making me tick. But since it was isolated as a chemical thing, they've been very, very supportive. They've been my major strength for the past seven years."

"I think it helped that my parents were both scientists," he continues. "My mother was a psychiatric nurse, and my dad's a biologist. They both saw what happened with my uncle with bipolar disorder, so they already understood what the illness was about. Once they had a label to put to what I was experiencing, they were very, very helpful and very, very giving. My mom would call me three or four times in the morning. She would return home and spend an hour and a half with me at lunch, and then she would come home as soon as she could. Not doing any extracurricular things at work so that she could spend as much time with me as possible. She's gone to every single psychiatric meeting with me. She's very proactive. She's always clipping articles about mental health for me."

"If you had to persuade someone bipolar to get treatment, how would you do it?"

"That's a tough one. I wouldn't want to scare them, but I couldn't lie to them either. I guess being afraid is a major part of accepting it. I would try and tell them that their personality is almost completely independent of the disease. The disease is not who you are; it's what you have to deal with. You can't really be who you are until you've dealt with it."

"What would your advice to parents be?" I ask him.

"I think it's important for parents to keep encouraging their kid to keep moving. Cause it's very, very easy just to give up and shut down. I remember there were times in high school when I couldn't even dress myself. My dad would tie my shoes for me and drive me to school because I couldn't drive myself. Keeping me in a state of motion helped me survive. All of that time when we were trying to figure out what the name of this disease was, I remember my parents offering to do my homework for me just to take a load off my mind. My parents initiated most of the contact I had with people. They kept me moving. That's very, very important."

Driving back to Atlanta, thinking about madness, manhood, and American society.

It never occurred to me before: bipolar disorder might be harder on men.

Draw a regular sexy man coming home from work greeting his lover.

Draw a regular sexy woman coming home from work greeting her lover.

Draw a sexy man suffering with an out-of-control brain greeting his lover. Draw him at work. With family. Draw the compassion he receives.

Draw a sexy woman suffering with an out-of-control brain greeting her lover. Draw her at work. With family. Draw the compassion she receives.

This whole week in Atlanta, I stay with friends of my parents, the Morningsides. Rob and Katherine have three kids: Alexis is off at art school in Savannah, Daniel is seventeen, and Henry is eleven. They set me up in an apartment in the basement of their home. I have my own bathroom, my own space, my own door to come in and go out. My room looks out onto their garden, and the walls of my bedroom are lined with books. I feel at ease.

They are away at school or work during the day, and I write and think. When they get home we hang out. They are smart and funny and totally uninvasive. Henry and I are best friends instantly. He's a skinny little blond wonder-being, chasing me around the house with original short stories and poetry for me to look at. We talk for hours and hours, imagining things, questioning things. He refers to me as the "psycho from the basement." Katherine shows me photographs Alexis took of Henry in tighty-whities with wings attached, frolicking in the garden. She won awards for them. They're fantastic.

Katherine's bipolar too, and she thinks Henry might be. He's been in trouble at school; the teachers say he has ADHD. Many people who are diagnosed with bipolar as young adults have been misdiagnosed with ADHD as children. Henry seems to be able to focus fine to me. He just seems brilliant and perfect, and his teachers probably don't know quite what to do with him. Katherine doesn't want to put him on meds, and I don't blame her.

Henry rules.

I tell her he's a genius and that I'll homeschool him as soon as I'm done with my project.

On my last night in Atlanta, Henry leaves the dinner table just as we've sat down to compose a poem for me:

> Field grass grows
> Swift but slow
> In a place where no one goes

Song birds sing
Rivers flow
In this place you find no woe
Down the river
Rapids rave
Splishing and splashing
Wave by wave
Mud of the earth
Sea of the sky
Listen to me, I tell no lie
There's gold in that land
But not the kind you hold in your hand
But gold for the nose the ears and eyes
This place is precious to only the wise

5

The Morningsides convince me to visit Savannah.

I stay with their daughter, Alexis. She's a senior at the Savannah College of Art and Design, which they call SCAD around here. She lives in a beautiful neighborhood; Savannah is full of them. Amazing trees, historic homes, verdant parks. Her apartment is huge with one bedroom, filled with art school girl stuff: a mannequin in weird underwear, shimmering colored curtains, naked self-portraits.

Alexis is great, and she's busy during the day, so I have the whole place to myself.

I have my journals.

I have time.

I have space.

Go ahead.

My parents say they knew I was having depressions when I was young.

My mother sent me to a psychologist. Because she thought something was wrong with me. I wrote this in green marker, January 31, 1984, at age eight.

I remember that psychologist. She was a friend of the family; she belonged to our pool club.

I didn't trust her. I had been caught, found out. I knew I needed to cover things up. This was around the same time my younger brother was born. My parents thought I was depressed because I wasn't getting all of the attention any more. I don't remember that being the reason, but I don't remember there being a reason.

I was a really sharp kid. I saw through every step the psychologist made. I knew where she was leading me, trying to see if anyone was molesting or beating me. I also knew she needed a reason, a thing to tell my parents, and that if somehow I could tell her an easy explanation for my sadness I'd get out of going to therapy, which seemed humiliating. Patronizing. Insulting. And dark: I really felt I was being found out, that this dirty and dangerous part of me was being revealed.

I told the therapist that I wished my mother spent more time with me. I was a manipulative little girl, and I knew to prey on my mother's guilt about having a busy career. My therapist probed no further and told my mom, who immediately set plans for the two of us to go sledding.

So off we went to the great big hill in our area to sled and bond. We had been sledding for ten minutes when I spotted a friend of mine and let my mother off the hook.

"But Lizzie," she said, exasperated. "I thought you wanted to spend more time with me."

"I only said that to get out of therapy," I told her.

I wonder what she thought.

But I remember being in school months later. A guest

speaker was visiting to discuss drugs or abuse or something, and I got up in front of my whole class, burst into tears, and announced that I was depressed and that my mom had sent me to a psychologist.

These public outbreaks, these strange darknesses—they remained in my parents' minds. Their friends would come over and be extra special nice; I didn't trust any of them. Their gaze was never innocent; it was always probing, trying to figure out where I was.

I was often sad. I didn't know why, and I didn't necessarily recognize it as sadness. I just felt I wasn't fit for the world and the world wasn't fit for me.

I would rather die than live, I wrote in brown marker, on April 1, 1984, at age eight. *If God would kill me in my sleep, I wouldn't care. I do want to die. I need help. Please, God, kill me. I might kill myself, but I don't know a good way to do it. I could take an overdose of aspirin. I do want to die. I don't care what people say. One reason that I want to die is that my life isn't going too good. Another is that I want to be with God. I just think it would be peaceful. If I could die, I would.*

In pen, April 20, 1984: *Hi again. I still want to die. I know I am going to have a bad report card. My mom will yell at me, and so will my dad, they won't let me do any more acting, and I'll be hated. I don't want tomorrow to come. My mom said she wouldn't want to live if I die but I don't care. I have an idea. I'm going to take an overdose of Nyquil. It's a sleeping pill. See, if I take ten tablets I'll fall asleep and never wake up. I'm serious about this. I WANT TO DIE.*

That was fourth grade. My journal from fifth grade is an incredibly detailed daily account of who I'm playing with, who I hate, who hates me, what gift I'm getting from Mom (*pink high top pumas, they're in style*), what's going on at the theater (*On stage I memorized my feelings: I'm gonna miss this show*). It's pretty boring. Every once in a while there's a short entry with an entirely different tone.

Like on January 2, 1986: *I'm gonna start my own theater. I'll use the garage. I'll write my own scripts, make my own everything.*

I'll sell lemonade for money. It'll be hard. But I'm sure I can do it!

I did. In my backyard I produced a variety show, which presented monologues, a dance I choreographed to Billy Joel's song "Pressure," and the premiere production of my first original play, *Rich People Are Mean.* It involved about a dozen or so of my friends and their younger siblings. I attracted over fifty people to my backyard to watch the spectacle, converting a space once specific to my brother's baseball games into a site-specific multidisciplinary performance piece. And I sold lemonade.

Was that a manic episode? I ask myself.

It was not an isolated incident. I remember staying awake for days on end as a child, inventing businesses, hatching plots, writing plays and books and songs. There was a greeting card scam once; I designed hundreds of greeting cards with my watercolor set and construction paper. I shopped them to gift shops in my neighborhood, searching for vendors who would display them to customers. I was nine? Ten maybe?

My parents saw my childhood bursts of energy and invention as evidence that they had a special child. They were entertained by it all; they assumed that I was just really precocious.

I know I was temperamental and intense. I know I was sad and desperate sometimes, and that when my moods swung too far to either side of the pendulum, it frightened me and made me alien to my friends and family. I know that it's strange to have fantasized about suicide since I can remember. But I don't wish I had been saved from growing up in this way. I don't think anything was really wrong with me. The world isn't set up for intense, sensitive, creative kids. I would have been a lot merrier growing up if it were.

Wait. . . .

I don't know what to think of seventh grade, when I attempted suicide for the first time. I remember taking lots of pills and then throwing them up. I didn't write about it. In the depths of depression I never write, only on my way down or during "normal" times. My journals show tons of ups and downs, dips and soars of self-esteem and popularity. This happens to girls that age in our culture. Maybe I was just experiencing preteen angst. Maybe I just wanted attention. Just when I'm ready to put the issue to bed I find scrawled across a page in the back of the journal: *God I wish there was some way for me to exit this hell I'm visiting.*

It was a bigger thing. I'm almost certain. And it traumatized me, growing up with this kind of uncertainty about myself. But what could anyone have done for me?

I remember one time my mom caught me crying myself to sleep. I was about twelve years old. She came into my room and lay down with me and asked me why I was crying.

I didn't know why I was crying. So I told her that.

"Well, what are you upset about?" she asked.

I didn't think she'd take another "I don't know."

"I miss summer camp," I said. I thought that would get rid of her. I didn't want her attention any more because I didn't have anything to tell her.

"That's not it," she said.

I was sort of surprised. She wasn't taking the bait.

"I'm flat-chested," I said. "And I hate it."

She bought that one, sympathized with me, told me how she used to feel the same way, and promised I would grow breasts one day soon.

I was a very sharp, mature kid. But I did not have what it took to say, "Mom, there is something wrong with me." My mother's communication skills are as good as they get, and she could not draw the truth out of me. If any mother-daughter team could have fleshed out the true nature of precocious melancholy, it was my mother and me, and we didn't.

It's. Just. Hard.

Stop. Just stop.

I feel *something* between me and the people I interview. It's not as strong as I imagined it would be, but there's something: a sort of force field that comes over us when we talk, which protects us. The environment tends to disappear, and it's just the conversation and the safety of the conversation. But it feels like four-in-the-morning drunk love patter with Genevieve or Garrett—sincere in its own way, meaningful and urgent, but safely inconsequential.

I'm feeling something, but it's not *the* thing. I liked Marissa, Jan, and Matt, I liked them a lot, but I'm not feeling the herd thing. I'm not sensing everything from my past clicking into place. I'm not feeling my brain and soul relax with the new spiritual community I've found. Not at all. They're just really nice people. The common bond I feel with them is big but not huge.

Wait. . . .

Maybe they're not successful enough. Maybe I need to find super-high bipolar achievers, people who are taking over, people who are on top of their game, magical wondrous bipolar beings. Maybe that's what I need to find.

I feel myself veering off on the wrong track. This isn't what I wanted.

I go to a meeting in Savannah in the hopes of finding an interview.

Again I'm in a big hospital complex, about fifteen minutes away from Alexis's. Driving to a hospital it doesn't matter what I'm playing on the radio: I feel shitty. I feel sick. I keep thinking about getting a drink. Isn't that odd? Would sure love to have a beer right now. Must get a six-pack on the way home.

Or I have flashes of having sex. I concentrate on where my legs are, or how fast Nick's going. Just to get me out of the moment I'm in.

These meetings are a bit too much for me, obviously, but here I am anyway.

It's seven, starting time, and nobody shows at Conference Room A, where the group is supposed to be. Just as I'm about to leave, a lazy-eyed blond lady with a slight mustache arrives. She's the leader. Her name is Lonnie. There are two other people with her. One is a guy in his late seventies named Kyle. The other is a 250-pound woman with an exotic manicure on four-inch nails, Larissa. Kyle is also a leader; he's got pamphlets with him.

It's a stale white room with two rows of desks and chairs. There's a projection screen and an easel with an oversized pad on it. Lonnie starts setting up the easel to use for her presentation. Kyle begins taking chairs down from on top of the tables. When he's done, he sits near me and pulls from his pocket his hearing aids, which he puts in.

Ms. Manicure sits beside me as well. She looks at me and smiles warmly. It's gonna be a long night.

I introduce myself to Lonnie. I tell her what I'm doing.

An ancient batty lady enters with a guy in his late fifties.

Lonnie is talking to me about my project, but she's not really getting it. Inside I'm pressing the pencil to the paper so hard the tip is breaking. She's telling me all about studies that are currently being done to prove that bipolar disorder is genetic. I

137

know the illness is genetic; I don't care. I go off in my head: I'm back in Schroon Lake with Nick.

"They're doing it on the Jewish people," she says, interrupting my chain of thought: "Not that I mean it like that."

Don't worry Lonnie, I think, I'm way too baffled to be offended.

So I'm testy. Don't know why. Maybe I feel that I'm wasting my time, not a young person in sight. Lonnie can't seem to understand that I'm looking for success stories. Yes, Lonnie, young bipolar people who feel great about life.

You know, here I am, and I call six or seven officials in every city I go to, and I'm just looking for one success story, and no one can seem to think of any.

And I'm tired. I have been hanging out with Alexis's friends, who are sweet and well-meaning but exhausting art kids all the same.

I take a deep breath and try to give the situation a chance. Lonnie is really trying to help me, and I feel guilty because I am talking to her as if she is dumb.

So I warm up. I half smile, the way it says to do in my Buddhism books in times of anxiety.

Soon another couple enters the conference room. They are middle-aged. They look like people I would see at the gym, you know, a dentist and his wife.

So there are eight of us: me, Lonnie, Kyle, Ms. Manicure, Batty Ole Lady, her middle-aged friend, and dentist and wife. No young ones.

Lonnie begins the meeting. She apologizes for not having arranged a speaker, but someone in her family had a heart attack and her house was broken in, and up! there she goes, she's off! in a mile-a-minute monologue about chaos everywhere in her life. Both of the policemen who came to the scene of the crime told her it was an inside job, and she only lives with her husband, and he wants to date other women and on and on and on. As soon as she starts into it . . . well, I've already explained where my mind would go to.

It embarrasses me when mentally ill people who are treated behave this way. It scares me. I want them to be cool and normalish, and then I feel guilty for being so intolerant and judgmental.

Next Lonnie explains that we're going to do a role play. She'd been fiendishly sketching a picture of a guy's face on an easel set and arranges the easel set before the group.

Role play.

This was something she learned in counseling, she says, and she is going to share it with the group. She marks different parts of his face: Head/Thoughts, Ear (Myself), Ear (the World), Eyes Looking In, Eyes Looking Out, Mouth/Expression. And then she lists different kinds of people: friends, neighbor, worker, family member, stranger, physician, psychiatrist, counselor, and in-law.

She's not making any sense to me, but I keep quiet.

So she tells half of us to pick part of the face to be and the other half of us to pick a person to be. She's going to match one person with one part of the face and the two will have to interact in front of the group while Lonnie takes notes.

"You're gonna be doing what's called improvisation," she explains. "It's gonna be like acting."

Kyle is really very old. Everyone talks loudly around him so that he'll hear. And when he talks, he never says anything that has anything to do with what the person talking to him has just said, but everybody pretends he has. I just sit and hope Lonnie doesn't partner me with him for role play.

We are all going along with Lonnie's game. People feel a little silly, but they participate. The Eye Looking Out talks to "the neighbor," and "the family member" talks to the Ear to the World. No one really knows what Lonnie is referring to with any of these terms she's learned in counseling, but we kind of do it anyway. We improvise.

When we're almost done with the role play, Lonnie tells us all about her cervical cyst and how doctors tried to prevent her from having a child because she's bipolar, but they left her cyst untreated and it became a tumor THIS BIG.

Nobody really talks at all during this meeting except Lonnie. So it's out of order when the totally ancient lady looks at me and asks me if I have ever been suicidal. And I say, yeah, I was. I probably tried to commit suicide a half dozen times when I was manic or depressed. I tell her that, and she tells me that her grandson, who's still struggling to find the right treatment, shot himself in the chest a year ago Thursday. He survived, and she comes to the group because taking care of him exhausts her.

Others in the group contribute anecdotes about their doctors. None of them get the kind of attention from their psychiatrists that they'd like.

"It's not an assembly-line kind of illness," says the dentist type. He asks me if people elsewhere complain about this, and I say yeah. I am sympathetic, but I have to be honest that my dad's a doctor and my grandfather was a doctor and thus I have had a life of perfect, affordable, careful treatment.

But actually, look what happened to me under the perfect conditions? I was misdiagnosed; I was misinformed; I was left to recover on my own, for the most part.

For these bipolar people, this meeting is a safe place where they can kinda let it all out. Lonnie says she feels as if she leads two lives: one in which people know about the illness, and one in which she never brings it up. "I have my three girlfriends, and we meet at the Waffle House, and we never discuss it. We just talk."

On the way out of the hospital, Lonnie promises again to help me find a young person in Savannah. She suggests Ms. Manicure, who is only twenty-nine.

Ms. Manicure says, "I don't know, Lonnie, I wouldn't call me a success," and she looks down at her nails.

Everybody in the group pipes in. "You're a success! Don't say that! Look how far you've come!"

"Wait," I say. "If she doesn't identify herself as a success, then she's not one."

The group falls silent. Ms. Manicure looks at me and nods. I'm a jerk.

Lonnie says that there are usually more people at the meeting, and she could put me in contact with George Johnson, who heads the Augusta chapter.

"I've already been in contact with George Johnson," I say. George Johnson is this LUNATIC on the register of a national mental health organization.

"What happened?" she asks.

"Lonnie," I start, "George Johnson tells me he doesn't have anyone for me to interview in Augusta, but he asks me how I am doing. And I think, aw, this is sweet, this guy's extending himself in a really humane way to a perfect stranger and I say, 'I'm great, I'm doing real well.' And then he says, 'How's your vertical?' And I'm like, huh? And he says it again: 'How's your vertical?'"

Lonnie smiles and looks at her feet.

I continue. "So I admit finally that I don't know what my vertical is, and he says, 'from your feet to the sky,' and I feel silly. He says, 'vertical is your relationship with God. How is your relationship with God?' he asks. And I say my relationship with God is fine. 'Then,' he says, 'you've taken care of your vertical. And the horizontal is life, and the two form a cross. As long as you stay on your knees and pray and read the Bible,' he says, 'you'll be OK.'"

I am appalled that this man is an authority figure, someone for those in mental health crisis to turn to. I almost said, "Yeah, George, I stay on my knees to suck cock!"

"George tells me he leads a group of seventy-five that meets once a month. It's probably some sort of cult."

"Lizzie, George is really important to a lot of people," Lonnie says. "You have to understand that below the Mason-Dixon line, it's the Bible Belt."

She then changes the subject and tells me she only has one working eye.

I can see my car now, and it's reassuring.

"Why is that?" I find myself asking.

"Well," she sighs, "I was a cashier at Shane's and we were held up, and the guy shot me in the head."

Now if my nana were here, she would say that all Lonnie needs is tight shoes, but I react sympathetically and become privy to all the gruesome details.

"I'm still known around here as the girl shot at Shane's," she says.

"Huh" is all I can muster.

The group goes out to eat after each meeting. They invite me to go, but I say I have plans. Plans to get wasted and forget that this ever happened.

I say goodbye and get in my car.

But I can't go back to Alexis's. I can't hang out with art kids right now. I want to be around other people, but I don't want to know who any of those other people are. So I go to Pinkie's Masters, a dive bar a short drive away from Alexis's. It's a one-room place with some booths and a jukebox. They serve me beer in small plastic cups. The bar is populated by couples. Everybody's watching the TV, which is over my head. I write, and I drink. A lot. I write twelve pages in a fury and get really lost on the way home.

In the morning I pack my things and call Chace Metcalf's mom back in Rhode Island. I have heard that he is at med school at Tulane, and I think it'd be interesting to reconnect and maybe stay with him in New Orleans. She gives me his number, and I call. He's super friendly and says that he basically lives with his girlfriend, so I can have his place all to myself for as long as I want.

Great. Maybe things will turn around. Maybe I'll find some people to interview, some special magical bipolar uber-siblings.

But there's something I'm nervous about. Chace doesn't know I'm bipolar, unless he's heard through the Rhode Island rumor mill.

I almost told him once. He visited me on Cape Cod the summer after I went insane. We had a lovely time together. The morning he left we went to the beach and sat on top of the dune, and the ocean was so beautiful that I figured the landscape was so gorgeous I could tell him something that personal and ugly, and the beach and the waves and the seagulls would make the conversation OK. I practiced it in my head over and over again as we sat there.

Chace, something happened to me.

Chace, I want to tell you something.

It just never came out.

I start heading to New Orleans.

I call over forty different officials from mental health organizations in Florida, New Orleans, and Texas. I'm pumped: I figure if I make all the calls at once, I'll be done, and the responsibility won't nag me over my shoulder all the time. And it gives me something new to do while I drive.

But it sucks. At about half of these places, I reach a machine and leave a message, the same message: "Hi, this is Lizzie Simon, I'm twenty-three, and I'm bipolar, and I'm working on this project to travel across country and interview people, young bipolar people, people between the ages of seventeen and thirty, who have been successfully treated with bipolar disorder and lead highly functional lives. I'm calling you because I was really hoping you or someone in your office might know of someone who fits those characteristics. If you think you might be of some help, I'd really appreciate you giving me a call back at 917-555-5555. That's a cell phone. Thanks a lot; bye-bye."

It is worse when I actually reach somebody. Over and over again, I hear people telling me they don't know of any success stories. Some go so far as to deny it is possible. "Well, I know people who do all right for a while," they say, "but they always go into remission."

Oh, sorry, did I say I was doing a project about TERMINAL CANCER? I must have slurred my words, I meant BIPOLAR DISORDER, a very TREATABLE thing!!

Sometimes their definition of successful frightens me. They'll start to tell me about someone who is doing so well that he can volunteer in their office once a week. Or they'll talk about someone who hasn't caused any trouble *lately*.

Now keep in mind: these are the same people you'd call if you or someone you loved were in crisis in this particular part of the country.

Don't you get it? I'm looking for lawyers, dancers, poets, businessmen. I'm looking for the chiefs, the sorcerers, the legends. Out of the dozens of phone calls I make, only a few leave me with some hope; only a few yield call-backs.

Today weighs heavily on me. I'm not doing what I set out to do. I'm visiting horrific meetings and talking to depressing idiots at mental health associations. I haven't met myself yet down here. WHY NOT? How do I?

I'm a superstar alien from another galaxy! Where is my herd?

It takes me four days to reach New Orleans.

I stop twice for meetings: once in Jacksonville and once in Tallahassee. But I don't encounter anybody I want to interview. They're all too old. And the bipolar people down here are an unhappy bunch. Stigma everywhere. They live in secrecy; most of their friends and loved ones don't even know about their experiences with mental illness. Their religious communities tell them that God will fix what ails them. The medical information they have is very poor. Their doctors pay little attention to them and encourage them to take few risks and keep life as calm and steady as possible, as if they are fragile dangerous beings.

These people are probably going to suffer for the rest of their lives, unnecessarily. I can't deal with the injustice of it. It's making me ugly. It's making me crazy.

I drive all day, stay in cheap motels on the road, and try not to think about how my whole project is getting screwed up, and try not to think about how I don't know how to fix it or save it, and try not to think about how panicky I am and how much I can't even eat any more because I am so nervous all the time.

In Jacksonville I stay in a nasty motel room. The place is for truckers and other dark-bearded, baseball-hat-wearing men. The walk from the check-in desk to my room is endless. It is the dream that you are walking through glue. The men are in the parking lot, staring at me, staring me down, watching me go to my room, watching me fumble with keys, watching me draw the blinds.

The wallpaper is peeling.

The bedspread is stained.

My cell phone isn't working, and I can't get through to the right people to fix it.

At least there's the motel phone.

I call Nick.

He tries to convince me to check out and go to a nicer place, but I am paralyzed and upset, and I can't muster up the organizational pull I need to execute that maneuver.

So he stays up all night long on the phone with me.

For hours and hours, until I am ready to move.

I get to New Orleans, and Chace has left a key hidden outside of his house. I find it, no problem, and I let myself in. Chace's home is a mini-house hidden from the street behind a great big house. He has two floors. The first is a living room and kitchen; the second is a bedroom and a bathroom. Every room is painted a different bright color.

Chace repeats that I can stay as long as I want. It's exam week for him, though, so he probably won't be able to hang out.

That's certainly fine with me. I just want to write and get my project into shape. I'm happy for the space and privacy.

Plus what would we talk about?

Chace leaves, and I settle in. I call my mother and tell her I am having a hard time finding subjects.

"You have to call your father," she says. "He knows doctors all over the place. He'll help you."

"OK," I say, uncommitted.

I don't want to call my dad.

I don't want to admit that things aren't going well.

I wonder if I could get my mom to call my dad.

I wonder if I could make do without dealing with either of them.

I fall apart a little bit and call him. We speak for a few minutes. He can't tell that I have been crying. He seems to want to be effective, so he suggests we get off the phone so that he can make some calls on my behalf.

When doctors begin calling me every fifteen minutes for the rest of the afternoon, I don't know whether to feel happy or guilty.

We're on campus, outside a small student center at a picnic table. It's late in the afternoon. Not very many people are around besides some skateboarders off to the side. Every once in a while somebody walks by who knows Madeleine, and they say hello to each other.

I found Madeleine through a doctor friend of my father's who works at Tulane. She's a very pretty young woman with freckled skin, delicate in some ways, with a wavering voice. She seems nervous. We talk about her school a bit. I ask her if she has any questions about me, and she asks me when and how I was diagnosed.

I go through my story for her fairly quickly. I've told it so many times lately. Then I ask her when she was diagnosed.

"The summer after my sophomore year," she says. "I was in ROTC, so I went to field training. It's four weeks; you go from five in the morning till nine at night. It's really strenuous."

"Is it all physical?" I ask.

"No, it's like boot camp, but there is a lot of strategy and stuff like that. It's for officers. There are a lot of leadership skills and games."

Madeleine is a soft Southern belle. I really can't imagine the boot camp girl in her.

"Basically I got there, and I was really scared about it. I really wanted to do well, because ROTC was something I was pretty good at in college. I've never had very good grades. I need five million things to make me focus on things for a short time. And bipolar people are all supposed to be smart."

"You're smart. . . ."

She shrugs. She's nervous. I had to promise her doctor a million times that I would protect her anonymity. He told me never to leave any telling information on her machine just in case her roommates heard it. I promised, but I thought for sure he was just being overprotective. When Madeleine and I finally touched base, I asked her if her roommates knew she was bipolar. "No way," she said. "NO," she repeated, forcefully, agitated. It's a big deal for her to be sitting out in public and chatting to a stranger about this. A really big deal.

But this all just happened recently for her.

"So I'm in Texas with people I've never met before. I went and I asked right off to be put as the leader of my flight, because if you can get that right off, then that puts you in a really good position. You're competing with the other thirty people in your flight and against the rest of the class. It's a weeding-out process."

"So people get kicked out along the way. . . ."

"No, it's not that many people get sent home, it's just all to see how you manage the stress."

This sounds terrible. Madeleine speaks slowly, so you can hear every creak and crack in her voice.

"I kept getting more emotional. I remember being really high strung. I couldn't calm down. I remember the sixth night, I just stopped sleeping. I just couldn't relax enough to go to sleep. That happened two nights in a row, and then by the third night I was freaking out because I couldn't figure out what was wrong with me."

"Nothing like this had ever happened before?" I ask her.

"Well, in small doses, but not for two whole nights. Especially . . ." she breaks and takes a deep breath so that she doesn't start to cry.

"Especially when I knew I needed sleep; it was so vital that I sleep. I knew I wasn't gonna make it if I didn't sleep."

"What did you do all night?" I ask her.

"I was thinking about everything. . . . At field training you do about twenty things a day. And you really have to get people together. So I was thinking about how to motivate people, thinking of really stupid stuff, like cheers. And I was going over better ways to go about things in my mind, going over mistakes I had made. For instance, you have to pass a physical test. The first time we went to go take that test, they weren't extremely organized because they were trying to do the whole camp of 240 people at once. So we got to one event, and there was nobody timing us, so I was like, well, I'll time! But I started early, and it ended up that they had to stop and start again because I was causing people to fail."

Madeleine 's face crinkles up, as if she's expecting me to let her have it.

"That's awful," I say.

"I was really upset about that. I got called out in front of the whole camp. I got yelled at, especially by one of the student officers, in front of everybody. I mean it's their job; they're supposed to do that. But then we were supposed to go to the colonel. We were supposed to march in front of the whole camp and tell him what had happened and apologize to the people who had failed in front of the whole camp. So we were marching over to the colonel and I'm crying. . . ."

"What happened?" I asked her.

"The colonel took pity on me," she says and gently smiles. "But that bothered me for a while."

"So you were really beginning to be out of control."

"Yeah, and it kept going. I was wired up. I kept going over the details of what had happened, just over and over again, working it and reworking it in my brain. And about the seventh day, I started thinking about this other cadet I knew who attended the year before. Now she was very built before camp. She went to camp, made it all the way through, graduated, and the next day she got home and she had massive body cramps because she didn't have any body fat left. She couldn't walk for six months. She had to withdraw from school for a year. And they couldn't figure out what was wrong with her. I started thinking about her constantly, as if that was going to happen to me. I knew that I was losing a lot of weight, and I guess I was paranoid about it. I hadn't been sleeping, and I hadn't been going to the bathroom. I had been really careful to keep myself hydrated: we were in Texas, and it was really hot. But I couldn't eat. And it wasn't that I didn't want to eat; we had eight minutes to eat."

151

I burst out laughing.

"What's so funny?" she asks, and smiles.

"It just seems ridiculous," I say.

She laughs with me. "There were some really good things about it, OK?" she says. "I'm only telling you the bad things."

"I wouldn't last a day in this situation," I tell her. No sir-ee. "Go on," I tell her. We're still laughing.

"And, you know, I was like this big trying-to-be-a-leader person. People were always asking me questions all of the time. I knew what I was talking about; I knew the rules sometimes better than the officers, so they were always badgering me. One meal, three different officers were asking me questions. But anyway, I really lost a lot of weight. I could tell by the way my uniform was hanging off of me. And in seven or eight days, you are not supposed to lose that kind of weight. So I went in and I told my officer how I couldn't eat and I couldn't sleep. And then I told my officer about this other cadet I knew about. Obviously he freaked out. So the next day I went to the hospital, to the med clinic on the base."

"But at this point it's not that obvious to outsiders that you're insane."

"Right. I mean, I guess. I don't know what people thought. I was trying to tell the doctor what was happening and I was kind of hysterical, probably in one of the best moods I've ever been in for my life. I don't know, the lack of sleep."

"Did you say *best* mood you have ever been in?"

"Yeah it was very strange."

"Well, you were manic."

"I felt euphoric. They really didn't know what to do with me. They made me eat a good meal. They went and weighed me, and I had lost ten pounds."

"Jesus Christ."

"The next day we were all in the auditorium. We were just having all of these lectures to learn about different officer stuff. Now, I don't know why, but I started thinking about about my dad. And I decided that my dad was suicidal and I needed to call him."

"Does your dad suffer from depression?"

"He was diagnosed with depression my junior year, after me. So there was some rational basis to that. But I got up in the middle of this lecture in this big auditorium, and you really don't do that. I was wigging out, and I went right up to the colonel who's sitting in the back . . ."

We start laughing again.

"And he's like, 'what?'"

"What'd you say?" I ask her.

"I just said I needed to call my dad. And eventually he got more out of me, but I was being really vague. So we go to his office and I call my dad and of course everything's OK. So then I sit down and they just know something is off. I talk to the colonel, who was a really nice guy, for a while, and I'm just going haywire. I don't even know what I said, and then the major came in to talk to me because the colonel had to leave for some reason. And I started to run off at the mouth."

We giggle.

"I don't remember anything about this conversation except for the fact that I was cussing. I apologized. I said 'Oh, I'm sorry' because you just don't do that. Like NO! That's like the epitome of disrespect. And he totally was OK and just allowed me to cuss, which was really strange. So I knew something was off."

"Were you still going on and on about your dad?"

"No," she says, and her mood drops. "Random things; I don't know."

"Do you not remember some stuff?"

"Yeah, actually . . . there was a whole week that I do not remember."

She looks at me.

"That happened to me, too," I say.

"Well, they took me to the hospital and tried to talk to me, but there was a week where I don't remember at all. I just remember singin' the whole time."

Madeleine cracks a smile.

"Singing?" I ask.

"I sang more country songs. . . ."

We start to giggle again.

"What songs?" I ask her.

"I don't know; I sang a lot of Reba McIntyre. 'Does He Love Me'—that song. But I do remember almost immediately people trying to tell me that I was bipolar. I didn't understand at all. I also thought I was a religious leader."

"You were gonna save the world. . . ."

"Pretty much, yeah. All the suicidal people were like my disciples."

We start laughing again.

"The worst, though, the worst, is that I'm slightly racist, so I'm not sure where I got this idea. Maybe it's just because I saw *Jesus Christ Superstar* and they represented Judas as a black man. But there was one black guy in the whole thing, and I started going off telling him that he was Judas. He was my downfall."

"Was he aware of what was going on?"

"I don't really know. By the time I left, he was my best friend there. I mean, I started to write a religious musical, and he was really into it. Everybody was, everybody got a part."

"That doesn't sound too bad."

"C'mon, Lizzie, I think it was one of the worst situations you could have put me in, that hospital. It was on a military base. All of the people there were suicidal, like ninety-five percent. They were really bad. What I realized later is that the reason why most people go into the military is that they don't have a lot of alternatives. They go to get away from their family, to re-establish their own independent lives or whatever. So they really didn't have anything else. . . . It took me a while to figure out what the scratch marks were on their arms. There was one guy that had horrible cuts on his wrists. He had cut himself in a Porta Potti."

Yuck.

"Eventually I just had to get out of there; I couldn't be there anymore."

After Madeleine was diagnosed, she returned home. Her mom took her to the beach for a couple of weeks to recover. She spent the rest of the semester working at the local mall.

Returning to school wasn't easy, and she still isn't sure she is ready. Because the military does not allow people with mental illness, Madeleine must let go of her former ambitions. And she wants to graduate on time, so she has a lot of work to make up. She picked a new major and a new minor.

And she started over.

Madeleine is into learning more about the illness. I recommend a couple of books to her and encourage her to seek therapy. I was going to encourage her to go to a support group meeting, but decide against it.

Madeleine breaks my heart. She feels she's let everybody down. She's certain her parents are disappointed in her. She feels she's made messes everywhere. She's about to graduate from college; it's a burden enough.

She's only seeing it as a series of horrible things she's done, even if intellectually she knows that it's an illness, that it's not her fault.

Life will begin for her when she doesn't treat every day like another opportunity to disprove the horrible things she thinks of herself. If I could give her anything, it'd be a truly clean slate. But as it is, I can't give her that. I can't give her anything. I just hope she feels that I understand what she's told me and that it makes it easier for her to talk about it in the future.

Madeleine is so deeply good, I can tell intuitively.

She just looks at me and cracks a smile.

I think about our meeting the whole way back to Chace's house, and when I get back there, I pull out my journals and my computer.

Madeleine seems really alone. Her friends don't really know what she's going through or what she's been through. She'd rather not talk about it with her parents because she wants them to feel like she's recovering. I didn't bother asking Madeline what her advice would be to parents and friends, what she thinks they should do to help the young bipolar person in their lives.

I'm starting to think it isn't about what they should do. What is there to do, anyway? It's how they could be. If parents could be any way we designed—if friends could be, if therapists could be—how would we design them, Madeline and I?

I'd put them there, here, right next to me, right in the middle of my loneliness and terror. I'd have them standing there or sitting beside me when the house is caving in and the ground is melting.

Parents, friends, doctors, whoever: DO whatever you like. Just BE there.

As soon as I have been back in Chace's house for an hour, I feel weird.

Really weird. Like CANNOT RELAX TO SAVE MY LIFE WEIRD. I really should get out and do some sightseeing. I've wanted to go to New Orleans my entire life, but I don't have the energy to figure out where to go. And I should be working on this project. I'm never doing enough.

I try to settle in. I make fifty or sixty phone calls and exhaust myself completely. Almost every single call leads me to an answering machine, and I leave my spiel, trying to keep it fresh every time.

I start thinking again. Chace was really nice and normal, and I felt so strange because I don't feel like he's ever met the me I am today. And it sort of kills me to think what he must think of me. He must think I'm such a weirdo. He must have let me stay at his place to have a weird anecdote to tell his med school buddies.

That's not even true. He was just nice and normal, as if I had always been nice and normal.

But, you know what, I wasn't nice and normal then—and suddenly I don't feel nice and normal now either. I was a freak. I remember. I'm sure he does too. I spent the year after we broke up crying about it in the student center bathrooms every day. I was a loser and an out-of-control weirdo, and he can play nicey-nice, but we all know what really happened. I was a weird girl. Who he made the mistake of dating.

You know all that stuff about hating my classmates in high school—it's all stupid. I just hated myself. Hated myself. HATED myself. I want to shriek right now. My blood is boiling. I just hated myself. I was so depressed and so desperate—of course I thought everything around me was dark and depraved. *I* was dark and depraved. I was such a loser, such an insecure freak. I would have done anything for Chace's love, for social acceptance. I was such a loser. I was so weak, and it's all still in me.

I burst into tears and can't stop.

And I'm in Chace Metcalf's house. What am I doing here? Why have I done this to myself?

I was doing so well with Madeleine. What's wrong with me?

I fall asleep, sobbing, exhausted.

When I wake up it's the middle of the night.

I think I'm having a panic attack.

I'm having a hard time breathing.

Oh God.

I need to get out of here.

I don't know where to go.

I hardly know where I am.

This isn't a bipolar thing.

I don't know what this is.

This is real.

I open my laptop and try to write.

The gray light settles the room a bit, settles my thumping inner thing.

You see, I write to my imaginary audience, *I am dizzy and my hands are shaking but I have work to do, like you.*

But I need to take time out because something is resisting my progress.

What is it?

Who do I hate?

Where do I funnel my anger?

At my meds? They are too easy to smash, and I need them anyway.

I resent them but I need them: they have saved me more than I have saved myself.

What kind of awareness is that?

What kind of integrity exists in that sense of self-sufficiency?

I'd be drooling or delirious or dead without my 900 milligrams.

But, never mind.

I am going to pass out soon, and I'm not wasting my time blaming the pills.

I can blame the illness, but I couldn't find the illness with a microscope if I tried.

I want to blame something I can bludgeon.

Of course there is something else to hate, to resent, to express rage at—and it's me, because it's my faulty body that's not handling this stress or this lack of sleeping or this lack of eating right.

During these moments, I want to spend the rest of my life safe, in a big sweater on a big bed with a big dog, waiting for a big man to return from work to give me a big hug. Because I am terrified at how disabled I can become, and how quickly.

OK, now. Easy there.

I try deep breathing.

I think I'm just upset and nervous and tired.

In . . . Out . . .

Eventually I fall back asleep.

I am awakened at five in the morning by my cell phone. There's a message that they are shutting my service off. I call the phone company, give them money from my credit card. They tell me it'll work in two hours.

I can't fall back to sleep, so I wait the two hours out.

When the phone isn't working two hours later, they tell me it should be working, and they don't know why it isn't, but to call back in an hour if it still isn't working.

It isn't.

I call back.

They're mystified; they tell me to call back in a hour if it isn't working.

It isn't, so I do.

But I lose my cool this time, and the lady hangs up on me, and I just start to cry again.

I really have to get out of here.

I can't seem to even pack, but I force myself.

One thing at a time, I keep saying.

I write Chace a thank-you note.

Takes me ten drafts, but I do it.

I call Nick on Chace's phone. I wake him up.

Ten seconds later he's promised to meet me in Austin, Texas, in less than forty-eight hours. His biotech company has an office there, and he's been meaning to get down there anyway, he says. I have the name of the hotel, its address, and a reason to keep going.

I get in the car.

I'm getting gas in Texas somewhere.

I have some fears about this project of mine.

I'm afraid of support groups. I'm afraid of the mentally ill. I'm afraid of how intense they are, how they so often seem haunted.

I'm afraid they'll be smelly, their hair unkempt and sticking to their heads. I'm afraid they'll speak and make no sense. I'm afraid the old men will hit on me.

I'm afraid of feeling sorry for people.

I'm afraid of being alone this much. I'm afraid my brain will collapse in on me from being alone so much. I'm afraid of falling asleep at the wheel. I'm afraid of my car being stolen, or my computer. I'm afraid of being really lost.

I'm afraid of the South. I'm currently in the South. It seems harmless for now, but weird. Just weird enough to be on the cusp of too weird, freaking-me-out weird.

I'm afraid of motels. I'm afraid of staying with friends of my parents. I'm afraid I don't know how to be a guest. I'm afraid of taking too much food at dinner. I'm afraid of sleeping too late, or not being able to sleep at all. I'm afraid my parents' friends will want to spend time with me, and I'll just want to be alone because I'll be freaking out.

I'm afraid of running out of money, of the New Year arriving and finding myself totally broke. I'm afraid of having to say, "Dad, I need some money." That would just suck.

We know what they're up to—what they're planning and what they are capable of—and we'll tell you this: It's no good.

ZIP!! IT!!

I'm afraid of obsessing about money for the entire trip and letting it affect me. Of doing stupid things that stress me out, like sleeping in the car or living on bagels—things to save money that would fuck with my head and prohibit me from doing my project right. Or it'll be this constant interior monologue about money, a constant brain calculation. I'm afraid I'm not cool enough to say to myself, you know what, kid, you've got ten grand and a car and an awesome project to tackle; just go for it, because you don't have any children and you're twenty-three and what was Bob Dylan doing when he was twenty-three—was he worried about running out of cash? I'm afraid I'll return to my job producing.

I'm afraid I'll give up on myself.

I'm afraid of some big mean wise person figuring out the big problem with my plans, pointing this out to me and demanding of me, "Didn't you ever consider this most obvious big thing? What exactly were you thinking?"

I'm afraid I'll fuck this up. I'm afraid I'll fuck this up because I don't have the confidence to do this. I'm afraid I'll get sick, or get so anxious I have to come home.

We bet within a week the walls are smeared and splattered with blood. . . .

WHAT!! EVER!!

I'm afraid of all of these pressures I am putting on myself, and I'm afraid of what I'll do to myself when I have nobody around to tell me to take it easy.

I'm afraid I got into this just because I didn't know how to quit a job everybody kept praising me for.

And now? And now? And now? What now?

I'm afraid I am changing, that this experience can not be unexperienced.

Just to be on the safe side, just keep them the hell away from us, OK?
SHUT!! UP!!

I am afraid that this is the dreary end to the intricate self-sabotage plot only I could have created.

My friend Speed Levitch would probably say that I'm just afraid of my own limitless power. He tried to explain to me that the only reason fear was in my life was so that I could conquer it. He said, "Lizzie Simon, DO NOT CONSPIRE WITH FEAR."

But I'm really afraid I won't find what I'm looking for. I'm afraid I won't find my herd. I'm afraid I'll be lonelier when I finish than when I started, and more confused about where I come from.

I'm even more afraid that it's not even a herd I need to find, that it's something else: something even more elusive than finding a herd with the same problem, something I'll never figure out, something . . . undoable, unfixable . . . I'm afraid that what I'll find is something just terribly horribly wrong, and rotten, and toxic.

I'm officially a mess.

I would like to announce my official failure. I would like to announce that I am way too fucking far from home. I would like to announce that I'm freaking out. I would like to tell the people that I have failed them completely and can no longer continue my project. I would like to admit that I am in no way smart or strong enough to do what I set out to do and that I am giving up. I would like to say that I no longer give a shit, that I'm tired of having so much fucking pressure on me all of the time. People of the world, adieu.

I'm closing shop. I'm taking a fucking vacation. Till when? I don't know. Till I feel better.

Full tank, I'm outta here.

I set Austin up to be my saving week, my re-energizing vacation.

It isn't that.

Maybe for a while it is—the first moments, at least.

I arrive in the room first, take a long shower, leap naked into bed, and fall asleep.

Nick stumbles in at two in the morning, and we explode.

We talk and mess around for fifteen or sixteen hours.

We spend three days together.

Nick has business during the day, so I occupy myself.

Wander around the pretty streets.

Take naps in a much swankier place than the motels I've been staying in.

Try not to think.

But you know, those little things.

Those little indicators.

Room service bringing Nick up a six-pack every few hours.

His frequent trips to the bathroom.

Something dies in Austin.

Something unfolds, and exposes nasty innards.

The smell of the rot grows until I have to deal with the dreaded moment: I can smell that smell.

I really can.

I do. I smell it.

It's real. It really smells.

The last night, Nicholas and I end up in the hotel lobby; we've been out late. I finally drag him back. There are these fancy people sitting there and drinking, and the bartender tells us that one of them is an astronaut and was one of the first people to ever go to the moon.

Nicholas decides to send him a bottle of champagne, and they invite us over to sit and drink with them. They are complete Texans in tuxes and gowns. One of them is playing songs on the guitar, and it's a sort of sing-a-long they've got going on.

Why are there so many songs about rainbows and what's on the other side?

This is fun.

Anyway, we head up to the room finally.

Nicholas goes into the bathroom for a while.

Then out of nowhere, he picks a fight.

I don't remember what about.

I get nervous because he's being such an asshole (screaming, hollering, red-faced, insulting son of a bitch), and I decide I'm going to leave.

This is all happening very fast.

He's just about to hit me or something.

My mind churns.

I know this isn't a safe situation anymore.

I really know.

My car's in the parking lot, I think.

I'll just go.

Head West, get back to the project.

Fine.

But this is my brain. My heart is dizzy on a tightrope.

Grab bag on left, go round the bed, dart to the door. Go.

Grab bag on left, go round the bed, dart to the door, GO!

GO! Come On!

GRAB BAG ON LEFT, LIZZIE, GO AROUND THE
FUCKING BED, DART TO THE DOOR, GET THE FUCK
OUT FUCK C'MON GO!!!

I start to move.

SLOW MOTION BLUR.

Nicholas grabs my arm and throws me onto the bed.

Nicholas grabs me by my arm

and I'm walking toward the door

but he's strong enough to throw me, to T-H-R-O-W M-E by
my arm,

his muscled arm and body lifting me by my arm

and throwing me

in the other direction than I was headed with my own quiet
force (his is stronger),

and he grabs my arm and throws me onto the bed.

It hurts a lot, my arm.

I'm scared.

I cry.

He comforts me.

We make love.

You get the picture.

I'm heading West, no particular destination in mind.

(Use this blank page to color a picture about a time you were freaking out so bad you couldn't even describe it to another person.)

For several days I drive and drive and drive, stopping for food and gas and for motels at night.

Driving feels different. My phone doesn't work. The voice mail is gone, too. So if any of those mental health association people call me back, they'll hear a message saying my phone is out of service. I doubt they'll keep trying. But I don't care. I'm done with this anyway. Did you hear that? I don't care. No more project. It doesn't matter. One thing matters. Matter matter, pitter patter. I matter.

Project Fuck You All, that's what I'm working on currently. Alert the press. Project Fuck You. PFU. That spells pheu. I am the president and CEO of PFU. Now go fuck yourself. Thanks.

Driving.

I call home from a pay phone, and my dad picks up. He wonders why I don't sound so good.

I tell him I haven't been sleeping very well at night, so I've been trying to compensate during the day.

The shame.

My father says you can't make up for lost sleep; it's a myth.

You can't make up for lost pride either,

for shame,

for bad situations you put yourself into.

It's a myth.

A fucked-up one.

You feel shame.

You try to correct it.

Undo it.

Force a better ending.

The cycle is endless.

You just have to stop.

STOP.

STOP!!!!!

WALK AWAY!!!!!!

Say FINE I feel shame.

There it is, over there, my shame about this situation.

Fine, there it is.

Loss of pride.

Shame.

Over there.

There it is.

It's okay.

It's what it is.

I'm at a truck stop in mid-Texas. They have phones at every counter. I buy some phone cards. I spend an hour on the phone with Sprint PCS. I get a different answer every time. No one knows why my phone won't work. I've paid my bills.

I call my mom, I call my cousin Julia, I call Genevieve and Garrett.

I don't mention Nicholas.

I tell them I am crushed that my research is messed up, that I am really beginning to have a nervous breakdown. I tell them I feel like a failure. I tell them I cry six or seven times a day. I tell them I am afraid of people. That my clothes are hanging off me. That I've lost quite a bit of weight. I tell four different people the same set of information, and they all think it's funny because I can't seem to cry for help without making it all into an entertaining anecdote.

There's a few other people in the truck stop, but I'm the only one talking in the whole place.

They think I am funny, too.

I am poolside in El Paso.

El Paso was the longest drive, and the most consistently beautiful. It's just all mountains and cactus. Are they mountains? I don't even know; it's all just one big scenic postcard of the West with a road running through it, and every half hour by the side of the road there's a small town about a half mile long, full of stuff you might need. And total Texans who stare at you but who are nice.

Today I feel better than I have in a long time. Even when I was crampy or thirsty, even when I had to fill up my tank three times in nine hours of driving, even as I was pulled over and issued a speeding ticket, even as I had exhausted all of my mix tapes and the radio played only one station and that was a country station and it was all songs with titles like "She Thinks My Tractor's Sexy"—even through all of this I feel better than I have in a while.

See, something huge occurs to me on the way to El Paso: *I could be tanning.* So I do. For a few days I tan, read fashion magazines, see movies, shop for soaps and candles, eat at nice places. I fantasize about a handsome cowboy riding into town and whisking me away to a more traditional life on the ranch. I do everything within my power to entertain myself.

And it hits me. If all I wanna do is meet and talk to people like me, I don't need to run around searching.

I'm wherever I go.

I can just sit down and start chatting.

Hi.

Hi.

How ya doin?

Good. How 'bout you?

I'm good.

Rough patch back there, huh?

You betcha.

Pretty dark.

Yeah.
You OK?
Yeah. You?
Yeah.
How 'bout this weather?
Can't beat it. I feel good.
I feel good too.
I think you're getting a tan!
Really?
Yeah!
Awesome! I love being tan!

And then one day I wake up with ideas about this project again. Lots of them. One day I wake up and the seventeen-year-old who's bugging me because she just came out of the bipolar fog is in my brain again.

My father's gang of doctors help me set up two interviews, one in Phoenix, and one in LA.

I set new goals. I will conduct two interviews and get the car back to Providence, taking care of myself the whole time. And that's it. And that's enough.

Today as I am driving through the canyons, from El Paso to Phoenix, I start to primal scream. It feels pretty good.

"This is my life," I screech, and I bang my fist on the armrest. "Fuck off!" I say toward the mountains, but probably to some voices in my head. "I'm tired of crying every day! This is my life!"

Today is the most beautiful ride. I loved the marshes in the south and the swamps around Louisiana. I loved all of those bridges heading for Texas that swept over so much water you couldn't see the land at the end. But today is just a fantastic nature show from start to finish.

And the canyons are gorgeous. They're sitting there where they've been forever, watching kids like me roll by, and they're like, yup, dummy, it's your life; take it easy, all right?

6

It's threeish. I'm outside of Rachel's house waiting for her to get back from school.

She's the real deal, Rachel, all sixteen years of her. She's the one I imagined I was doing the project for.

I'm trying to remember the last time I sat down and talked for a couple of hours with a sixteen-year-old. A long time ago.

I feel really steady, well rested. It's strange: I feel sweet. I haven't felt this way in a long, long time. Back in New York, I was so hardened, so tense when I was producing, and so isolated. Everybody around me seemed to need something from me, and I just turned off, stopped being a kid, stopped being tender with people.

The house is in an upscale neighborhood in Phoenix. I set the meeting up with her mom, who was really enthusiastic about my project and about Rachel getting the chance to talk to with me. She's pulling in the driveway now with Rachel in tow.

We meet and step inside.

As it turns out, Rachel is a cute young Korean woman who doesn't know she's attractive yet. She goes to a school where boys are only into blond girls who play field hockey. She's got that teenage-girl-discomfort-with-her-body thing, and she speaks in this sardonic tone.

Her mom is a very pretty blond. She's warm and welcoming, and she fixes me a glass of ice water before Rachel and I shuffle off to the living room for privacy. Rachel seems really unsure of what she's getting into. I try to seem bubbly and easygoing.

I complement her on her shoes, and we begin. Rachel was adopted from Korea when she was six months old. She's got an older brother and sister, each of them adopted from different families at different times. Her brother is seventeen and schizophrenic. He lives at home. Her sister is in college and will be twenty in January.

"Did you and your brother realize you had mental illness at the same time?"

"Not exactly," she says. "It wasn't until last year when they diagnosed him, and they diagnosed him not too long after they diagnosed me, which was really hard on my mom. They diagnosed me with depression in eighth grade. And then manic depression at the beginning of sophomore year."

"What made them diagnose you bipolar?"

She looks at me slyly. "I had . . . a very interesting summer."

We both break into smiles.

"What happened?" I ask her.

"I don't know. I had failed algebra, so I had to retake it in summer school. And summer school was just a really intense atmosphere . . ." she pauses, and looks to the side. "The main thing was a shopping spree," she says.

"What'd you buy?"

"Like, a lot of clothing from various different places. And I never used any of it. I just bought stuff and it sat in my closet. Cause I felt bad . . . I mean, I took the money from other people."

"You mean you stole money?"

"Yeah."

"From who?"

"Um . . . Well, like my parents, obviously. But other people that I didn't even know. My mom has a business right now, so there are like . . . Master Card and Visa numbers . . ." Rachel is uncomfortable. "So that's what I did. Oh, and I also got way paranoid about weight. I lost fifteen pounds in three weeks. That was fun."

"Was your mind sped up?"

"Sped up? Oh yeah! That was the other thing. I was in summer school and all of a sudden I was a genius in algebra. So yeah, it was really interesting, from failing to, like, really smart in algebra."

"So it just sort of came to you, like, oh my God what have I done?"

"It kept piling up."

"How many different people's credit card numbers did you steal?"

"Six total," she says.

"All at the same time?"

"In the span of a week. On the internet."

"Oh."

"Yeah, so that was good."

"Did you think you were going to get caught, or were you just not considering it?"

"I was afraid I was going to get caught. . . . I don't know, I don't know why I kept . . . I don't see how . . . there's a lot of like guilt and stuff. You know how you feel like you've gotten in so deep you can't tell anybody?"

I nod.

"So that's what I felt like, so like, if I ever told anyone they'd kill me, but of course they didn't kill me when they found out. But my mom thought I was . . . criminal, or whatever."

"What happened to the people who you stole from?"

"We returned all of the merchandise, because you know, I didn't open it, so it was really easy to send back. So nobody found out."

"They didn't find out?"

"It was done in the less than thirty-day policy."

"So none of them even know that it happened."

"No. I could be in jail right now."

"Your mom helped you cover your tracks."

"Yeah, my mom and dad."

"So there was the stealing, and the being a genius in algebra."

"And sleeping. There was like, no sleep. Constantly awake. And the weight loss. And that's still not a totally gone away problem."

"What's that, your weight stuff?"

"Yeah, dieting crap. It's better. I didn't throw up or anything; I'd do one of those huge binges and then starve myself for a while to make up for it, to make the numbers the same. I don't do that any more, really. I have to keep to a strict schedule. I guess schedules are good for people with manic depression."

"So what happened; they diagnosed you?"

"Yeah, I went to this psychopharmacologist, and she was really good. Telling her was hard, but like, she knows. She said she'd heard a lot worse. But she told my mom my diagnosis two weeks before she told me."

"How does that feel?"

"Well, I didn't know until she said your mom already knows. I'm like, wait a minute. I was so pissed."

"Why were you pissed?"

"Cause she told my mom before she told me! And like my mom's sittin' there at dinner, and I'm sittin' there and she knows that I have this. I was so mad."

"Did you tell your doctor you were pissed?"

"Yeah. I was so mad. I mean, you tell my mom before you tell me?"

"That's really disrespectful."

"Yeah. I still think that; I don't understand. They said it was too much too handle or something."

"Well, not knowing is a lot to handle."

"Yeah, I guess it was to help her prepare for when I found out, because she got to go the library and do research."

"I guess. . . . Have you ever been violent, Rachel?"

"To myself, yeah. I scarred myself."

"Were you trying to hurt yourself or kill yourself?"

"I don't know. . . . There are some days you do not want to get up. You know . . . you think, I'm going to hell anyways, I might as well make it faster. You feel like you're totally alone. There's no hope. Nobody understands you. Once when I was really little I was really mad about something, and I went into the medicine cabinet and just went right across and took one pill after the other."

"How old were you?"

"Six."

"Wow."

"Yeah, I mean, I was showing a lot of signs from a very young age. My mom didn't know I did that. I just threw up the whole thing."

"So what are you on?"

"I'm on Wellbutrin right now for the depression part and on lithium for the manic depression. I wasn't always on the Wellbutrin; that's new."

"Are you planning on staying on your meds?"

"I never had a problem with that, actually. There was a slight temptation at first, because one of the side effects was weight gain, and I was just like, oh, my god. I've been battling this thing and then they tell me I'm gonna get fat. I was like, that's not gonna help my moral psyche, getting fat. So I was like, which one, fat or sane. I think I chose the right one, cause one's easier to fix than the other. . . . No, I've never gone off of it. If I did it's because I forgot."

Rachel and I talk about how destructive the illness is and how much safer and confident we feel on medicine. "Freshman year sucked," she says. "It was a waste, the year of waste. It's messed up my transcripts. I keep taking summer school, because you can take a class over in the summer and it will replace the grade on your transcript. So I've been doing that for the past few summers, making up for my freshman year. It's really funny: these girls in my school are like, 'I'm so depressed,' and I'm like, 'oh yeah?'"

"I know a lot of people who are older than you are, Rachel, and who are older than I am, and it's one thing to trash your freshman year in high school but it's another thing entirely to trash a career or a family. People do that, you know. People twenty years older than us, thirty years older."

"That's what everyone says to me, that I'm lucky."

"Yeah, you must want to tell everyone to fuck off."

"Yeah, I do. But seriously, I do think I'm lucky. I mean it could have been my first year in college or my first year out of college."

"Yeah, I mean it's hard to think of a year more insignificant to the rest of your life than your freshman year of high school."

"I am thankful, I guess. I haven't had it so bad."

"It must be hard to relate to the people in your high school."

"It is because you hear things. Like I had to watch *Disturbing Behavior*—have you seen that movie?"

"No."

"It's got all of those people in it, like Katie Holmes. There's a scene in a mental hospital, and people are distorted and clawing and that's like, pounding that image into their heads. I mean, it's messed up. I was prejudiced against people like that, and then I become that? The first thing I said when I was diagnosed as bipolar was 'Oh, my God, I'm one of them?' One thing that was helpful: we had to give a persuasive speech in school, and I did mine about stigma, so I had to do a bunch of research. I think that helped a lot."

"And you did this in front of other students?"

"Yeah, I did it in front of my whole class of like thirty-two people."

"Oh my God. Do people in your high school generally know that this has happened to you?"

"No way; there are only two people that I've told."

"And you know that they're never going to tell anyone?"

"Yeah. They're both guys; they've both been through a lot. But at my school, I'm already different. I'm one of ten Asians in a school of over two thousand students."

"So you are an alien."

"Yeah, and I'm adopted; that's also weird. Basically from fourth grade to the beginning of sophomore year, I hated being Asian. I bleached my hair—anything to look white."

"You actually dyed your hair blond?"

"No, I tried bleaching it, but it didn't work. Also, with eye makeup. Let me just tell you, you are so lucky to have an eyelid. You don't even think about it! Then one day you look at yourself and you realize that's the difference between my eyes and everybody else's. And you figure out how to help it with makeup."

"You have to go to New York. You'd be the unfreakiest person there."

"Yeah, in San Francisco and New York, Asian women don't wear eye makeup! But in high school, white guys don't go out with Asian girls."

"Oh God! You're gonna have such a great life when you get out of here! They'll be lining up around the corner for you! I can't believe guys don't go after you."

"No, they don't. Everyone wants to be in a cookie-cutter couple. In my high school, one mistake and you're down. If the girls in my school ever found out about my being manic depressive, I'd be out. They'd make my life hell. I mean, I'm not friends with them, I just hang out with them because they're there. It looks bad when you just hang out with guys."

"When were you first aware of your differences?"

"In seventh grade. I don't think I thought before seventh grade. I started thinking then. I started wondering why I felt like crap and why I felt so different. Before, I thought that everybody felt like that. It is so weird. They put me on the Wellbutrin only after I told them that not a single day had gone by that year where I hadn't felt depression. I thought everybody felt it, though."

I just can't believe she's sixteen. "So you've already started over a couple of times?"

"Yeah I've had two start-overs."

"And you're off to college soon. Are you afraid of the transition, being on your own?"

"No. I mean, I'm afraid of what will happen because every time some big transition has come up, something bad happens. Like the change from sixth grade to seventh grade—that was major. I was like 'Oh my God I'm out of my classroom of thirty people to a class of six hundred, following bells, and at lunch time you don't play around the playground any more; you have to hang around and talk.' Then from eighth grade to high school, all of a sudden you're around eighteen-year-olds. I'm actually looking forward to going to college. I'm pretty sure nothing's going to happen, but it's just that every single time I've changed school or routine . . ."

"One of the women I interviewed said she felt like everybody was given a handbook when they were born on how to be and that she never got one. Do you feel that way?"

"Well, I don't feel like everyone got one," she says. "I mean, I don't think anybody knows how to be. Even the people who act like they know everything, I know they don't know everything. But I do feel like we have to take the long way. We don't have the straight . . . you know, we have all of these barriers, we eventually get there, but . . . that's what I think."

"How do you feel now?"

"A lot better. But have you ever felt like you had a false personality? Like sometimes I think, is this pills, or personality? And then some people say the pills just bring out the real me, but I don't know which one it is."

"I don't know either, but I can tell you that every bipolar person I have interviewed has wondered that same thing"

"Yeah, totally. I was just saying I question it. I don't care that much any more. As long as it does its job. I'm just happy that they found it, and that I finally have an answer for past stuff. People can forgive me for a lot of past stuff now."

"Would you say you're hard on yourself?"

"Um . . . for some things I still feel bad, like things I said to my parents."

"Yeah. One of the things that I'm trying to focus on in this book is what went right with people who are all right. What went right with you?"

"What went right with me. . . . Yeah, I guess I'm high functioning. Well . . . I understand people better. I don't understand the situation, maybe, but I understand what someone's feeling. And that's gotten me a lot of friends. Because people weren't willing to listen to me, I'm willing to listen. Also, loyalty—I've got a lot of loyalty. Because some family members were really willing to dump me, and it made me really loyal."

"I meant something different. I meant what about you made you get through this? Many people don't. But what helped you survive when things were terrible?"

"Well, I always felt like I owed my family, because even though they weren't understanding what I was going through exactly, I always knew they were trying. They were trying as hard as I was, in a way."

"I think it's family," she says again. "If I didn't come from such a strong family, I don't know if I would have gotten through it. Even though I still hate my mom sometimes when she doesn't let me go do stuff, and she's so strict, whatever, I'm not allowed to ride in anyone else's car. But I got my permit and stuff, and I'm gonna get my license."

Rachel smiles mischievously. I think we're done.

We smile, and I wrap things up with Rachel. I give her my phone number in case she ever wants to talk to another bipolar person.

I have a feeling she won't use it, but I feel good knowing she has it.

Nick and I have let a week or so pass without speaking. We leave each other voice mails, but we manage not to actually connect.

When I finally speak to him, he tells me he has been in some trouble, that Jenny said that he slammed her head into a wall in a drunken fury. He doesn't remember it happening, but he believes her. He is working on repairing their friendship.

The news cuts; it's scar red, blistering, permanent. I could maybe pass off what Nick did to me in Austin in the hotel room, but here was Nick himself, admitting it, saying out loud: I slammed her head against a wall.

This relieves me of thinking I had provoked Nick by being someone he felt like hurting. I've had it all warped in my head.

Jenny's perfect, I think, and he hit her.

But there's more bad news.

Joe's dead; he killed himself. Joe the hot-shot agent bipolar friend. Nick's freaked out. It's a big deal, on the cover of the *New York Times.* And Gary's in trouble, too, he says, but he won't go into it.

Maybe, I think guiltily, if Gary tumbles too, Nick won't think it's so cool to be so reckless.

Nick says he finally went back on meds but then jetted off to Boston immediately for a Tornado concert. He said he puked for three hours straight from whatever his doctor put him on. I don't really buy it. He met a Harvard student in a bar, and she let him sleep on her couch.

Nicholas will always find somebody to help him, won't he?

I have worried about him from the moment we connected. For what?

He's not even really trying to get better, is he?

I'm not perfect at all, I think to myself, but I wake up and I try, and I have every day since I was little.

I can't save him. I'd like to stand by him until he's better, but I'm not sure I can do that either.

In 4-D, he's my prince, my warrior, my angel. But as mortal beings living one little moment at a time, Nick is a mentally ill coke fiend, resisting treatment to both conditions. It's really hard to dress that up.

And his world is only darkening as days go on.

Sara is twenty-nine, a graduate student in art history. She's a stunning woman with doe eyes and high cheekbones. She has a great figure. She dresses in hip clothing. I am a ratty kid next to her.

We meet in front of the Los Angeles County Art Museum, where she's been doing research. We decide to get brunch nearby. On the way there, she tells me she didn't sleep much last night because she was out. She tells me a funny anecdote about running into Drew Barrymore in the bathroom of the bar they were at. I'm happy she's cheery and chatty.

This'll be like girl talk, I think.

I ask her what nationality she is.

"I'm Armenian Russian. I came here when I was about six, when I was in second grade. My mom is half Russian, half Armenian, and my dad's totally Armenian."

"And when were you diagnosed?"

"Well, I had my first breakdown when I was fourteen, actually."

"Wow, that's young."

"In my ninth grade, I went to this crazy school where everyone was, like, a drug addict, total rebel; it was such a contrast. I think that change was really hard for me. I was so sheltered and innocent, and everyone was having sex and doing drugs. It was like a rich kids' rehab school. I went there because my best friend was going there. And my parents are immigrants; they didn't really know much about the different schools."

"What did they do for a living?"

"My father was an art dealer who had a gallery for about thirteen years. My mom was a professor of languages in Armenia, and here she helped my dad with his business."

"Do you think anything in particular triggered your breakdown?"

"I don't know. My whole life has been kind of hard, so I don't think that any one thing made me break down. . . . I've had a lot of family problems; my parents hated each other, constant bickering and fighting. I was pretty unhappy in general. I couldn't wait until I was eighteen so I could get out of that home."

"Did you get along with them?"

"I got along with my dad. I have the most perfect relationship with him, almost too perfect. I don't think we've ever had a fight in our life. Total opposite with my mom. I couldn't stand her; it was miserable. I would dream about them getting a divorce and my mom moving out of the house. And by the time I was eighteen, they had gotten divorced."

"What is she like?"

"Well, she has this; she's bipolar. I get it from her. But she's never been treated, and she doesn't admit to it. She's also got a lot of delusions, conspiracy theories, a lot of anxiety—things that I'm not plagued with. I'm strictly bipolar; I have nothing else going on. Mine is so easy: I take Depakote; that's it. I think it's rare. I don't know many bipolar people who only take one drug. The minute someone complains about something, they give them a prescription for additional meds."

"I only take lithium. I've been on the same dose, same drug for six years."

"Me, four. I don't even feel like I'm on anything."

"Me neither. Do you still feel like you cycle?"

"I do get depressed."

"Like normal people depressed?"

"Yeah, but I think I cycle, all of the time."

There's a levity to this conversation. We could be talking about anything. "Could you tell me all of your bipolar stuff in order?"

"That'll make it easier. I had that first depression when I was fourteen. Through talk and . . . just . . . cycles, I came out of it; it passed through me or whatever. And then it didn't happen again for nine years, until I was twenty-four. Isn't that weird?"

"Yeah."

"And in the meantime, my family went through hell. My father lost his business. I withstood it all really well."

"That's really interesting."

"But in the back of my mind I always knew I was susceptible to something. I didn't know its name, but I figured, well maybe it won't come back."

"What about your mom? Did she say she related to you?"

"Well, it took her a long time to admit that one time she had a catatonic breakdown in her twenties. But she's highly functional; she's got a Ph.D. She's a very brainy person, but in real life she has no common sense. She can't even boil an egg type of thing."

"Do you resent her for not dealing with it?"

"I did resent her because she didn't share her thing with me for a long time, which could have made it a lot easier for me to understand. I wouldn't have felt so alone. You *get* this and you think you're the *only* person in the world. You were young when you got this, too. You don't know about stuff like this, right? You just think you're crazy."

I nod. "Where were you working when it happened?"

"At this really prestigious gallery in Beverly Hills. I was selling art. One day I went rollerblading and fell down and hurt my tailbone, and I had to lie down, and as soon as I lay down it was like everything slowed down. I was like that for a couple of days, but then I couldn't get up. I started not talking again and I was like, 'Oh no, it's happening again.' Total flashback. I couldn't talk. I had a complete shutdown. A complete and total shutdown. I went to live with my aunt because my mom certainly couldn't help me. She was freaking out. They took me to a county psychiatrist; he put me on Haldol. Have you ever *had* Haldol?"

"I can't remember, but everybody hates Haldol."

"You're drooling; you're pacing. It's the most disgusting drug you could ever take. It's used a lot for schizophrenia, and I think they misdiagnosed me or something. Anyway, a year of experimentation—I felt like a guinea pig. They put me on every drug on earth, except for the ones I needed. Finally they gave me Prozac, and I went through the roof. The most drug-induced mania. That was scary."

"What happened?"

"I had so much power, these delusions of grandeur. I was so powerful. I was so invincible. I was so *warped*. I don't even remember parts of it. I went shopping, spent thirty thousand dollars on credit cards. . . . No credit anymore, needless to say."

"What did you buy?"

"Everything, anything, clothes, ridiculous things. I kept giving it away, I'd see a bartender somewhere; I'd give stuff to her. I just bought and gave away. I didn't even keep anything. Three weeks before I got sick, I had met this guy, Roy, and we started dating. He has ADHD, so he really knew about this disorder 'cause he's done a lot of research, and ADHD and bipolar people have similar symptoms sometimes. And he was like a godsent angel. He took a leave from his job for six months and was just with me. I'd get up at four in the morning and just walk around the street because I was so hyper. He felt so bad for me; he felt someone needed to take care of me. We're still great, great friends. . . . You don't give someone up like that! Even if it doesn't work out, you don't let them out of your life. That's really amazing, that someone after three weeks of knowing me—I mean, my family couldn't even do what he did."

"That is amazing."

"I remember walking on the beach with Roy, and I told him I could see myself floating into the ocean and never coming back, and he was like all right, get into the car. I mean, at that point he knew I could just up and throw myself into the water. Poor guy. One time, when I was manic, he gave me his credit card, like, 'Honey, here, if you want lunch, use my card.' This is after knowing me for two weeks. So I took his credit card and ended up buying him ten thousand dollars worth of art. And then I go to the jewelry store and buy myself five thousand dollars' worth of jewelry. He didn't realize I was getting sick. We had to return it, but it took him a year of fighting in court to get the money."

"That's charming behavior."

"I know. Imagine that—he's still my friend. Can you believe it? I knew the jeweler, so he took it back, but Roy felt so bad for me. He was like, 'Honey, I can't afford this.' I felt bad; I wasn't thinking; I was just walking around charging. He was so sweet: he was like, 'You can keep one thing,' and I kept this ring."

It's gold and elegant with several small diamonds. "It's beautiful."

"He was so sweet, he was like, 'I want you to have something.' It's funny because it looks like an engagement ring. I never take it off, because it reminds me of a time when someone took care of me when I needed someone so badly. If I ever believed in God, I believed that he was a godsend for me. I don't think I'd be alive; I really don't. I was so dangerous. I was in the middle of traffic, thinking 'Oh my god I'm up, but I'm gonna come down again.' The only thing that kept me alive is that I felt someone cared about me. It kept me grounded a little bit. He would talk to me all the time. He was the one who educated me about this, and who diagnosed me. He was like, 'Get off that Prozac; you're bipolar.' I stopped taking it and went to another doctor, and he was right. He would get on the internet and print out all of this stuff for me. He'd say, 'Read this and read that.' He ordered books for me. I mean he was very, very caring."

"Why did you guys break up?"

"Well, after six months he was exhausted. He had to go back to work. And one day he was like, 'Look, I'm going to be working twenty-four hours a day. I need to make up for this time.' His credit cards were maxed. He was feeding me breakfast, lunch, and dinner."

"Were you devastated?"

"I have never been dependent on anybody for my whole entire life. Not my parents, not my boyfriends, no one. I've been more of the caretaker, always. I was very sad, I cried. But I totally understood that he needed to go, and I wasn't going to give him a hard time. I was not going to drag it out. I totally left him alone. He's definitely one of the most amazing people I've ever met."

Sara and I talk for a while about men and dating and wanting to get married and raise a family. Like Marissa, Madeleine, and Matt before her, she's got major fears about having children. She's heard encouragement and discouragement. She's worried about what being on meds would do to her child in utero, but she's worried what being off meds would do to her in the world. Her parents have told her it's a terrible idea. Most strongly, though, for all of us, is the anxiety that our child might be bipolar, too.

Sara turns our conversation back to boy talk. "Besides Roy I haven't had a real relationship in seven years. I think that's another thing the illness does to you, because you don't want to attach yourself to anyone; you don't want to deal with more loss. You know how much you feel. I mean, I think I feel so much more than most people do. I feel everything more. I feel more love, I feel more pain, I feel MORE."

"Were you ever promiscuous?"

"Oh yeah. Before my big breakdown, that summer I slept with five guys. That's huge for me."

"Were you going to bars a lot?"

"Yep."

"You felt more attractive than usual?"

"Totally. I could walk up to some superstar model and be like, 'hey, what's up?' I thought I was the hottest thing ever."

"I've never slept with anyone when I was manic, but when I'm feeling manicky I always feel like guys are more attracted to me."

"Well, your energy field is so up, and people are so attracted to that. That's why my sales would skyrocket."

"What was the best day you had in sales?"

"My first week at work, I sold thirty thousand dollars."

"They must have thought you were a whiz kid."

"They were like, 'you're great.' I did it all myself. I closed the deal. And I didn't know that much about what I was selling. Picasso prints, Chagall prints, etchings, some commercial stuff, that Beverly Hills caca that people put in their house. People who have money but don't really know much about art. I could talk you into anything. Make you fall in love with the art, make you fall in love with me. I was so exuberant.

"And then a month later, I couldn't talk. It was so weird, because it happened to me at work. People would come in. . . . You're supposed to talk; you're supposed to explain the painting. I just looked into space. I couldn't say three words about the work. Customers were looking at me. They would say, 'What does this painter do?' and I would just say, 'He's from Paris.' One day, I just walked right out of work. I didn't say good-bye or anything. And I never went back. They kept calling me. They were, like, you know, 'we like you, what's going on? Take a few weeks off. Did we do anything?' And I can't talk. My mom's like, she's not well. And they were like, 'What do you mean she's not well? What does she need? A few weeks off? A month? What does she need?' My mom was like, 'I don't know, she'll call you when she's better.' And I never called them."

"That's so humiliating."

"Yes, Lizzie, it is. One thing I have to mention is . . . that I felt so much *shame* in every place that I was where I broke down and people saw me. When I bump into people that have seen me . . ."

"Going back is so. . . ."

"It is so painful."

"I know."

"It is so painful. I still can't cope with that. I see people that have seen me, and I know that they think I'm a freak. And I feel like why should I have to prove anything. I get almost angry. Why do I need to prove to them that I am not insane, that I'm OK, that I'm normal? I don't even want to go there. I'm like, I don't even want to know you. I don't even want to say hello to you. I don't even want to know you exist. I know that I am being judged in a really harsh way. It's not kind, it's not compassionate. It's very negative, and that's just part of the consequence."

"How was your relationship with your doctor?"

"I met the greatest doctor in the world. I had had so many horrible doctors, and I felt like he gave me my life back. I had such an amazing relationship with him. I didn't even feel like he was my doctor because he talked to me like a total normal person. We were like, friends. Rare, amazing man. I think I had a crush on him. I felt so connected to him; I've never felt that connected to anyone in my life."

"Wow."

"I just felt total understanding, total compassion. One of the most brilliant and intelligent people I've ever met. He never treated me as anything less than his equal, which is amazing, because I am not his equal in mind or knowledge or anything. He's brilliant. He introduced me to a lot of Buddhist philosophies as well, because he thought I would find it interesting. The Dalai Lama's sister had come out here for a lecture he organized, and he invited me to that, and I really got into it, and it's brought so much peace into my life."

I half smile.

"You know? I thank him for that too, because that's a lot, you know? That's a lot to give someone before you send them off. I got a lot out of that relationship. I feel really blessed. If everybody could have a doctor like that, they'd be so much better. I only took my medicine because he was my doctor."

"Wow."

"I trusted what he said. I really blindly trusted anything he wanted me to do. I don't feel that way about my parents, or my boyfriends, or my friends. And he got me to go back to graduate school. I didn't really have faith that I could do it. I was afraid I would fail again. I was so sick of going to a workplace, staying for six months, and either having to quit because I was so sick or being let go. I've probably quit seven jobs and was fired twice. I should have been fired more often. Every time you do that you feel like you've failed in a way. And I was like, I don't want to start school and not be able to finish it. I already have a degree; I don't need a master's. I don't want to fail at this, and maybe I can't do it. And he was like, 'Of course you can do it. You can get your master's or your doctorate. You're everything you've always been. You can do it; you can do it.'"

"Do you ever think, what if this was fifty years ago?"

"I think about it all the time. I also think, what if Depakote didn't work for me, I'd be in a mental hospital. I mean there are people for whom nothing works, and there aren't that many drugs for bipolar illness."

"I know. I feel lucky—I mean I take my three pills before I go to sleep. Game over; that's it. Whatever side effects I have are totally manageable."

"Totally. I don't mind being bipolar. I would mind if there was nothing to help me. But I think I'm a more interesting person for it. If my personality's intertwined with it, I wouldn't want to change it, because I wouldn't want to change my personality. If I were going to be any different than I am, if I were going to be not as intense of a person? Forget it; I like it."

"Awesome."

"I think there is no possibility of having it not shape your character, though. It's even hard to separate if this is your personality or if this is your disorder. I'm a very extreme person: is that my personality or is that my disorder? I don't know."

"Pretty much everybody I've interviewed talks about it."

"I think it's intertwined. It's a mood disorder, but one of the things it does is make you a highly sensitive person."

"But maybe just highly sensitive people get the disorder?"

"I don't know. Had I had a really normal family and regular life, I don't think I would have been bipolar. Even my doctor said that, because my episodes were so severe."

"But it's genetic. It doesn't matter if your family's messed up. My family gets along, and I'm bipolar."

"Really?"

"Yeah. Plenty of bipolar people come from regular homes, whatever that means. I mean, conversely, everybody's got fucked-up shit in their lives, and they're not all bipolar."

"I will never know. What my doctor was trying to explain to me was, if that gene hadn't surfaced then I could have coasted through life with ups and downs. Once it breaks and you fall apart," she continues, "you have it more severely. It's like you're glued back together, but that part of you will always break with the slightest. A lot of people have this genetic makeup, and they don't take medicine, they function, they don't have it as severely. The more bipolar people I meet, the more I realize that they are all completely different. Some can't do anything, some do so much. Don't you find that?"

"Absolutely," I say. "But I think there is a direct relationship between how functional someone is and how repressed the person is in our society vis-à-vis mental illness. In other words, the most functional people have totally beaten stigma down, and the least functional people have been beaten by stigma. I think stigma is a much more important indicator of someone's success than the degree of their bipolarity, although I don't even know how you would begin to measure degrees of bipolarity. But I think that all bipolar people could have highly functional lives if certain societal improvements were made and if they all had access to proper treatment."

"Yeah, but in the end you've got to do it all yourself, for yourself. My family is still totally in denial. They all hate that I have it. I mean, my dad loves me to pieces, but it's even harder for him. He asks me every month, 'So when are you going to stop taking your medicine?'"

"Oh, God."

"He's like, 'Well, you're better now.' And I'm like, 'I'm better because I take this.'"

"He doesn't understand it's a chronic illness?"

"Where I come from people don't understand the concept of chronic illness. You take medication to get better, and then you're better. I mean, I think it's a symptom of the Western world, too. I think people are overmedicated. Over there, you don't always pop an aspirin every time you have a headache. You have to be bleeding to be sick. And they've seen me licking the floors—do you know what I'm saying? They've seen me in a mental institution."

She continues. "I feel like I'm such a disappointment sometimes. My dad has always thought I was perfect. But I've totally disappointed him. To maintain a normal life for me now, I have to live an average life. I can't be overly ambitious."

"Sure you can. You can be anything you want to be."

"Maybe you can, Lizzie. I don't mean average in a bad way. I mean I work eight hours a day type of thing. I have a balanced life. I can't be an overachiever, which I was when I was younger. I can't have a stressful job where I'm going to be making $200 thousand a year because that'll kill me. It kills most people anyway, but I can't take that kind of stress. I can't work and go to school at the same time."

"Are you sure?"

"Yes, I am positive. I am. Every time I take on a load like that, like I took on fifteen units and got to midterms, and then I crashed. I need to rest; my body needs rest. I've already tested this out on my body. I always pay the price."

Sara and I have exhausted each other. We've been talking for three hours. I thank her for her time, and she thanks me for brunch.

"You and I, I think we're gonna be all right," she says. We exchange phone numbers and go our separate ways.

The sun is setting in LA, and I'm getting out of here.

And it's not because I'm unhappy or dissatisfied with my research; it's because I got what I wanted, and I'm free to go.

I finally feel comfortable doing what I set out to do. I call my mother on my (YEE HA!) working cell phone. I tell her I think I'm catching on to my method, my process. She says that's great, that I should do another road trip in the spring, now that I know how to do it.

I just pretend she didn't say that.

I head to the Grand Canyon for a private celebration.

I spend the day wandering around, driving to different points.

There are families and couples and church groups.

Europeans and retarded children and Brownie troops.

Sororities and Mexicans and retirees.

I sit down on the edge and peer out.

After a while, I begin to feel high.

The canyons communicate with me:

You're in charge, they say.

We trust you.

We know you know how to get things done. How to make attention for yourself and how to retreat.

You can eat when you're hungry and sleep when you're tired. You know how to shower, and clean up, and pay your bills on time.

You know how to say no and how to say yes and when to do both.

You can let the right people in.

You can show the wrong people out.

We know you can ask for help. And for company.

You know how.

This is an adventure. Your adventure. You can enjoy this.

You have the power to forgive yourself.

To stand by yourself.

To be close to people.
To cry all you want. We don't care.
You have all the wisdom you need.
Just listen harder.
Look more closely.
You're in charge.
We trust you.
Now go home.

part

7

Heading home. I'm heading to my parent's home, where I haven't spent more than three days since I was eighteen. Toward the biggest messiest burnt bridge I have ever created. To a place where my family has been hoping for a real homecoming for six years. To a town where I have failed at homecoming over and over and over and over again.

I am committed to making it work. I am overwhelmed with how much maturing I feel I must do in order to be truly free. But rejoining my family seems like the obvious first step.

I'm going to try and contribute something to them besides heartbreak and turmoil. I'm going to try and have a real conversation with my father every day. I'm going to let my defenses down with my mother. I'm going to be a real sister for my little brother. He's going to learn to count on me. I'm going to show them who I am, and I won't have what I do to hide behind. I'm going to let them enjoy me, and I'm going to try my best to feel safe in their house. In our house.

And I'm going to drive by my high school and see it for what it is: prime real estate.

But I'm still currently in the state of Colorado, so I still feel OK.

I wanted to find a herd because I wanted to be close to real people in an honest and deep way, because I simply had never been able to sustain that kind of rapport with anyone, no matter how much I longed for it. My whole life I've been this way, from birth, from scratch. I imagined that the reason why I could not connect with people was that they weren't bipolar. And I don't know how much that has to do with bipolar disorder, but I am beginning to understand how it is all connected for me in my own life and in the lives of the people I interviewed, who each reported loneliness and isolation.

I'm also thinking about this obvious habit I have of not letting people, particularly men, know that I live with a chronic mental illness, even if they've proved to me that they dig me, even if I'm not involved with them romantically. I saw it on this trip—Chace, my boss Jim, Davide—and I heard how other bipolar women report doing it. This obvious thing I do, this obvious picture of cuteness I try and hold up: Blech. I need to give the men in my life a chance. It's boring and it's getting in the way.

And I'm thinking about how I've been on this road trip for six weeks in a literal way, but for six years in a very real way as well. I'm thinking about the fact that every single time I've been in a bookstore over the past six years, I've gone to the psychology section to see if there are any new books on bipolar disorder. And for the most part there haven't been. I'm thinking about being in college, and taking the subway for an hour and a half to a part of town I've never been to before, to go to a support group meeting for bipolar people. And not meeting anyone young. I'm thinking about looking up research in the library about bipolar people and seeing that they've only used a dozen subjects on a study as important as whether or not lithium hurts a fetus in the mother's womb. I'm thinking about how I studied revolutionaries and radicals for four years at Columbia, trying to find a blueprint for the survival of my spirituality. I'm thinking about the intimate journeys I've made with people, trying to create an understanding between us, trying to understand and be understood. I'm thinking about all the people I sought out because I felt their waters ran deep, and I'm thinking about calling them when I get home.

And starting over again.

I didn't find my herd. I didn't. I will probably keep in touch with the people I interviewed; they are lovely inspirational people. But I won't be scouting for real estate for our commune any time soon.

I did listen enough to understand my brain better. I did pay homage to the terror I've experienced since I was a little girl. I did see self-doubt and self-hatred enough to see it in me for what it is. I did want to scream *give yourself a break* so much to the people I interviewed to start kind of whispering it to myself.

I didn't discover my herd; I discovered that finding "like kind" isn't a solution in and of itself. I figured out that if I find myself desperate for people to stand by me, than it's likely I'm not giving myself what I need. And then I discovered recovery through tanning and magazine reading and empty-head time through beautiful vistas. It's compassion for myself that I discovered, through compassion with Nick, Marissa, Jan, Matt, Madeleine, Rachel, and Sara. It's no herd, but it's a huge discovery.

My experience as a bipolar person has been my navigation system, my lens to see through, my motivating fuel, my 4-D glasses. For six years it has brought me all over the place, but I'd like to put it to rest. I'm tired of being on the road, tired of having one foot out of the door, tired of not having a community or a real home. Something happened in Texas when I stopped searching, when I made my top priority to be OK in my body and in my mind in that moment on that day and every day henceforth. I don't know what it is, or what it was, but I feel that something large in me has changed. I'd like to think this trip will be over when I reach the East Coast. I know it won't be. But it will be different. It already is.

Home.

If you grew up feeling unwelcome in your home, you experience a spiritual homelessness which becomes part of your identity. It's with you whereever you go.

According to the young bipolar people I interviewed, their families provided them unconditional love but not unconditional trust. Trust couldn't survive the disruptions and heartbreak of mental illness. Trust couldn't rebound completely when diagnosis and treatment brought peace and security.

I could recognize this tension in my subjects' stories like road signs on their highways. Big, and looming, they had *issues,* obvious ones, teaching me where they were at and where they could go.

All the people I interviewed were making different kinds of efforts to be part of their families in a healthy and positive way.

Their efforts inspired my own.

But things are really different after my detour, mostly because I am ready for them to be different. I feel a solid foundation within me; I remember the canyons.

I am ready for my family. Bring them on.

In me, there is seemingly no hostility, no sense of doom. This time, home is mellow and warm and even a little boring. I actually look forward to giving guests tours of Providence and to listening to the wacky adventures of Brown alumni.

The house is also new to me. My parents relocate every few years, and they moved into this quaint Victorian home about a year ago.

This new house lets me start over in it.

My life is simple. I am working on the transcriptions of the interviews, eating meals with my family, and going to bed early at night after watching TV.

No deadlines.

No openings.

No cast parties.

No shows to see.

No people to call.

No bills to pay.

No social life.

No men.

Except my dad; my little brother, Ben; his friends from school; and occasionally my older brother Aaron.

Ben and I haven't really spent time together since I was a teenager, which is stupid. I was never avoiding *him*.

He is a quiet kid, a good-looking and sensitive sixteen-year-old. He doesn't speak unless he has something specific to say. And he doesn't seem to have much to say to me specifically at first. As time goes on our conversations develop.

It is my job to drive him to school at eight in the morning and pick him up at six. Eventually, he talks to me about girls and pot and music and what his friends are doing.

I actually hang out with his friends. His best friend is Teddy, an exuberant and gregarious redhead whom we call Annie.

"How many pages did you write today?" they ask me, grinning, after school, and I tell them "Seven" or "ten" or (sullenly) "none."

At first I was sort of terrified of them: these huge, tall, soft and awkward things who speak a strange language together. But they are so harmless is what I discover. It makes me think about all the "adult" men I know and how they're just strange guilty innocents on the inside, just sixteen or so still, but dressed up.

Ben, Annie, and I go to the movies or rent videos or get pizza or go to school games.

I watch a lot of their basketball games. Aaron drives in from Boston and watches them with me. My brothers and I go out to dinner afterward and hang out and make fun of one another, and Ben's this prep school jock, and Aaron's this stockbroker, and I'm this—who knows what I am—and it feels new and old, but good.

I am practicing a new way to be.

As for my parents these days, I just try to relax as much as possible and not be in too big of a rush to bond and be normal. They have always wanted to be close to me, and they always possessed the maturity to know how much I was a victim of my moods, even before they knew my diagnosis. They have been ready for me to "come home" since the first time I "went away" as a child. In many ways, rebonding with them is less complicated than rebonding with my brothers.

Generally, it is easier to reconnect with my mother than with my father. My mother and I have always had a close, though frequently testy, relationship. She is outgoing and craves intimacy. In her own life, she probably has four or five intense conversations a day, minimum.

My father is quite different. He took me out to Chinese food for lunch the first day I was back, and it was awkward, like a date, both of us trying to tell entertaining stories. There was raw energy in the air, that dizzy feeling of being on the edge of a top of a high building: *woah, vertigo, my dad is someone I barely know.*

But then it got so normal. My dad would come home from work for lunch, and I'd be watching VH-1 (I'm sure he suspected I wasn't working on my research at all, because whenever he came home if I wasn't watching VH-1, I'd be sleeping) and we'd talk, just really casual talk, like talk between two people who are in each other's day-to-day lives.

My father is far more private and distanced than my mother. It goes against his nature to instigate emotional conversations, but finally I was comfortable enough to tell him, (in one of the most difficult interactions I have ever started), that I wished he would. I sat across from him and told him that I wanted him to know me better. Insofar as he actually and frequently attempts meaningful connection with me *against his shy and pragmatic habits to behave otherwise,* he has demonstrated a willingness and courage to know me that far supersedes that of any other human being.

My family is, of course, the original herd. They were the herd I'd always had, and when I was done wandering, they became the herd that welcomed me back. For that I am truly blessed.

The stories you write as a seven-year-old are strangely powerful.

I now see in Elmer's creator a tremendous faith in her protagonist elephant: that he was an elephant who could lose everything but be OK, an elephant who would survive castigation (Get Lost!) through creativity (one day he got an idea), courage and faith (he would start walking), and perseverance (and keep walking).

Going crazy is a detour, a journey outside the prescribed path. And making my trip was a detour, a voyage that wasn't going to build my career as a producer, but one I expected would make me a stronger freer human being when I returned to my career as a producer. This is one kind of detour: a path different from the normal but that lands you back on your original road. Another kind of detour happens when the road you turn onto moves you in such a way that you decide not to go back to the road on which you started. I expected my cross-country experience to be the first kind of detour, but in fact it was the second. I don't think I will go back to my life as a downtown producer. Experience changes you. My future is wide open.

Experience changes you. Detours are important.

Go on; get moving Elmer.

Get an idea in your head and wander.

Go on, Elmer; keep walking and seeking.

Get lost and get found and keep going on and on.

last words

When I found out that *Detour* would be published, I contacted my interviewees to let them know. Marissa had bought a house and had begun to work on a writing project on her off hours from work. Jan was still working as a DJ and had just completed recording a CD of original songs she had written. Matt was still living and working outside Atlanta, and all was well. Madeleine graduated from Tulane and was teaching dance at a camp her first summer after college. Rachel is looking forward to her freshman year of college, and Sara is finishing her graduate thesis at UCLA. I was worried that one of them would be in the hospital, or even worse off than that. But they all reported feeling better, stronger, and more relaxed than they were when they first met me.

Their updates were wonderfully life-affirming. People who dedicate themselves to personal growth do grow, and they get to enjoy their work almost every day of their lives.

Nicholas is still (despite a million interventions on behalf of his family) a drug addict. According to research, as many as

207

sixty percent of bipolar people suffer with drug and alcohol addiction.

It took me a very long time to let go of our relationship, even with all of the danger and destruction and emptiness he showed me. Nick is into freebasing and heroin now. Gary Angelone is in jail for fraud, Rick moved out of the penthouse, and neither he nor Jenny speaks to Nick anymore. My brother is still his investment banker.

Nick and I keep in touch, but only once in a while, and I maintain my distance. He writes me love letters over the internet every time he is trying to clean up his act.

I love you immensely. Don't be afraid of me anymore. . . .

It just makes me lie in my bed and cry and cry and cry.

I still feel great magnetism with Nicholas Berenson. My only kryptonite is this book, which reminds me of the truth.

Everybody I interviewed for this book is diagnosed with bipolar affective disorder, between the ages of sixteen and thirty-five, on medicine, and highly functional in society (with the exception of Nicholas Berenson). According to the most recent surgeon general's report, seven percent of Americans have mood disorders.

You wouldn't know by looking or talking to any of these bipolar people that they have had the pasts that they've had, unless of course you were looking at them and asking them the kinds of questions I did.

Everybody has stories about being dangerously violent or insomniac or paranoid or immobile. Everybody has tales of being reckless with shopping, or sex, or drugging, or whatever. Some of us have memories of all these things.

Most of us have been superhuman: seen things, done things, made things, achieved things no regular person could do. Everybody has had some other horrible traumatic events happen.

Everybody has lost faith in everything they thought was sacred, and then regained it in a new, more informed way.

Everybody wishes someone were to blame for this.

Everybody has stories about alienating their friends.

Everybody has stories about exhausting their parents. Everybody has somebody who loved them unconditionally through the whole damn mess.

Everybody has stories about being misdiagnosed, mistreated, misunderstood, and disrespected by the medical community.

Everybody has spent long stretches of time as zombies waiting for medicine to work. Most of us have been good sports about humiliating side effects like weight gain, bed-wetting, and drooling.

Everybody experienced a time when it didn't look as if they were gonna make it. Everybody did make it.

Everybody feels lucky to be alive. Everybody has survived an illness that is often fatal.

Everybody in this book has said in some way, "Hell no, I'm

not gonna sit on a couch and cope. I'm gonna get out there and rock the mic!"

Everybody feels lonely, but everybody isolates themselves. They always have, and they still do.

Everybody feels alone, and they're not, but they are.

Everybody has some people they tell and some people they don't tell. Everybody fears stigma.

Everybody self-medicates in some way or another. Everybody did before they were diagnosed, and everybody still does.

Everybody has read the same two or three books about this illness, because that's all that's out there.

Everybody is sure he or she experiences existence on a higher level than people without brain problems. Everybody feels anointed, chosen.

Everybody feels they're only halfway to where they want to be. From this group, I believe that everybody's gonna get where they want to go. And far far beyond.

Everybody I interviewed for this book is diagnosed with bipolar affective disorder, between the ages of sixteen and thirty-five, on medicine, and highly functional in society. We do not share the same illness, for we each experience it differently. But we do share the same diagnosis. And we share the same nagging inner voice that wonders: how much of me is me, and how much of me is this illness?

This is our interior, private response to the exterior, public noise of stigma. What does this thing "bipolar" have to do with all that I am and have ever been? What does it mean I will become, now that I am medicated? And what do I have to do with all that they say mentally ill people are? Do I have any relationship at all to other bipolar people?

Mine is an American identity crisis, born at birth, raised over time in countless experiences of alienation and insanity, brought to fruition at the height of my acceptance in society, and explored and exploded most recently as I drove my father's sports utility vehicle from Providence to California and back just months before the passing of the millennium, scouting for like kind, searching for my herd.

Bipolar people need to fight for good health care, accurate information, and proper cultural representation. We need to examine every single way that society's common sense about the mentally ill is affecting us and determining our future. Then we need to blow our noses really hard and get all of the societal snot out of it. All of it.

But wait, we can't stop.

We young bipolars, though we may be protected from episodes through meds, we feel with certainty that something has been taken from us. But when we investigate our memories of mania and depression, when we look back to see just how and just when and just who—where, even—we are, tumbled into the dryer, wrestling about with other problems, mitigating circumstances, false diagnoses, false memories . . . all we want is to look back, to see it clearly, and to find within these recollections clues, directives, evidence that might lend guidance for our present and future investigations.

This is complicated, but it isn't gobbledygook. We're looking for what's missing. And we were at the scene of the crime when all of the robberies took place, but we are unreliable witnesses. Our memories fail us: another reason to be disappointed in ourselves, another reason to rely on outsiders, another reason to decide for the sake of peace and progress, to stop looking back.

But we must investigate. We must never rest easy, feeling stolen from. There can be justice for us, too. So we must go forward with our investigations, and we must look back: first at our episodes, and then, courageously, at everything else.